in his own words

BRUCE SPRINGSTEEN

John Duffy

OMNIBUS PRESS

Copyright (c) 1993 Omnibus Press
(A Division of Book Sales Limited)

Edited by Chris Charlesworth
Cover & book designed by 4i Limited
Picture research by David Brolan

ISBN: 0.7119.3017.1
Order No: OP 46902

Exclusive distributors:
Book Sales Limited,
8/9 Frith Street,
London W1V 5TZ, UK.

Music Sales Corporation,
257 Park Avenue South,
New York, NY 10010, USA.

Music Sales Pty Ltd,
120 Rothschild Avenue,
Rosebery, NSW 2018, Australia.

To the Music Trade only:
Music Sales Limited,
8/9 Frith Street,
London W1V 5TZ, UK.

Photo credits: All Action: front cover; Glenn A. Baker
Archives: 64, 73; Larry Busacca/Retna: 29; E. J. Camp/Retna
74; Andrew Catlin/SIN: 4; Joe Dilworth/SIN: 81; Gary
Gershoff/Retna: 69; Steve Granitz/Retna: 59; Larry
Hulst/Retna: 51; London Features International: 6/7, 9, 16,
18, 19, 22, 30, 32/33, 35, 36, 37, 39b, 40, 44, 45, 47, 48, 49,
52, 53, 54/55, 62t, 65b, 66t, 67, 70, 71, 80, 85, 87, 89, 92, 94,
95; Janet Macoska/Retna: 20, 21, 66b; Robert Matheo/Retna:
56; Michele Matz/Retna: 58t; Barry Plummer: 50, 60, 72; Neil
Preston/Retna: 26, 38, 62b, 78b; Mike Putland/Retna: 12, 13,
14/15, 25, 27, 28, 75; Duncan Raban/All Action: 78t; Aaron
Rappaport/Retna: 82; Relay: 3, 6, 10, 17, 34, 39t, 41, 42, 43,
63, 65t, 76, 79, 84, 88, 91, 93; Debra L. Rothenberg/Retna: 5,
58b, 83t&b; Paul Slattery/Retna: 23; Bob Sorce/Retna: back
cover, 57; Rocky Widner/Retna: 31, 61, 96; Mark
Wyville/Retna: 77.

Printed and bound in Great Britain by Scotprint Limited,
Musselburgh, Scotland.

A catalogue record for this book is available from the
British Library.

CONTENTS

INTRODUCTION

"But he doesn't say very much."

True, unlike most performers who cheerfully galvanise their career through a string of pithy, flamboyant quotes, Bruce Springsteen says very little. He would rather his music and lyrics relay his artistic and thought processes. Obviously, the complex machinery of pop stardom (and an ever expanding media) does not allow even its most celebrated offspring to actually say nothing, and, down the years, Springsteen has had to face microphone and notebook like all the rest.

His reluctant comments, gathered here in one concise volume, make fascinating reading, perhaps by virtue of their scarcity. He doesn't waste his time making ostentatious or arrogant remarks; he talks about matters important to him - the records, the songs, songwriting, performance, the fans - in other words, the REAL elements of rock music, not the hyperbole.

At times he contradicts himself or is ambiguous but more often the prevailing impression of Springsteen is of a thoughtful, passionate and sincere man.

Obviously, a collection of quotes can only draw a sketch of an individual or a performer. They leave no room for the nuances of a smile or frown, the manner and style of the interviewer, the ambience of the place where the interview was conducted - all important factors.

As sketches of Springsteen go, however, this one is perhaps more vivid than any other. After all, it is all his own work - just like his music.

NEW JERSEY &
THE SPRINGSTEENS

*New Jersey's a dumpy joint.
I mean it's okay, but every
place is a dump.*
1974

My father never has much to say to me, but I know he thinks about a lot of things. I know he's driving himself crazy thinking about these things. And yet he sure ain't got much to say when we sit down to talk. 1974

See, I never had a record player for years and years. It was a space from when my parents moved out West and I started to live by myself, from when I was 17 until I was 24, and I never had a record player. So it was like I never heard any albums that came out after 1967. 1974

The student body at college tried to get me expelled because I was just too weird for them I guess. 1975

For six years my mother and father and sister have been following me around, trying to make me come back home. Every time I come into the house they say, 'It's not too late, you could still go back to college.' 1978

My father, he used to give me a hard time all the time, he never used to let up. It was always, 'Turn it down, turn it down, turn it down'. So tonight, I've got three million watts. I'm playing a hundred times louder than my stereo ever was – and he comes to see me. 1978

My father was a driver. He liked to get in the car and just drive. He got everybody else in the car too, and he made us drive. He made us all drive. 1978

I lived half of my first 13 years in a trance. People thought I was weird because I always went around with this look on my face. I was thinking of things, but I was always on the outside looking in. 1978

In the third grade a nun stuffed me in a garbage can under her desk because, she said, that's where I belonged. I also had the distinction of being the only altar boy knocked down by a priest during Mass. The old priest got mad. 1978

When I was a kid, I considered myself till I was 13 like the body was presumed dead. I was funny. I was the kind of kid that never got into trouble, but trouble would gravitate around me – not even serious stuff, only ridiculous kind of things. I didn't have anything to hold on to, or any connections whatsoever – I was just reeling through space and bouncing off the walls and bouncing off people – until rock'n'roll and the guitar. 1978

Asbury Park is still the same as it always was. If you got enough gas in your car you carry on to Atlantic City, if not then Asbury will just have to do. But it will always be my home. I like Arizona and Holland. London's pretty cool too. But I'll never leave Asbury. 1978

My mother was just like superwoman. She did everything, everywhere, all the time. 1978

There ain't a note I play on stage that can't be traced back directly to my mother and father. 1978

I was there (Parochial School) eight years. That's a long time. I still remember a lot of things about it. But I don't remember anything nice about it, so I guess I didn't enjoy it. It has nothing to do with me. I'm not involved in it. I'm here to play music; I'm in a rock band. Some people pray, some people play music. 1978

I hated school. I had the big hate. I remember one time, I was in eighth grade and I wised off and they sent me down to the first grade class and made me sit in these little desks, you know, little chairs. And the Sister, she said, 'Show this young man what we do to people who smile in this classroom' – I was probably laughing at being sent down there. And this kid, this six-year-old who has no doubt been taught to do this, he comes over to me – him standing up and me sitting in this little desk – and he slams me in the face. I can feel the sting. I was in shock. 1978

There's this smell of religion, this smell that convents have, well, every time I went there (Catholic School) I got sick, I just threw up. 1978

The old priest got mad. My mom wanted me to learn to serve Mass but I didn't know what I was doing so I was trying to fake it. 1978

My father used to drive around in his car and it would not go in reverse. I remember pushing it backward; that was just something you did, you didn't even think it was strange. 1978

One day my father said to me 'Bruce, it's time to get serious with your life. The guitar thing is okay as a hobby but you need something to fall back on. You should be a lawyer, they run the world.' 1981

I was like nowhere, on the outs. I had no choice, that's where I was, that's where I got put, that was my place in life all the years I was growing up. I did a lot of running away. And a lot of being brought back. It was always very terrible. It started when I was in sixth grade. 1981

We had a bathroom with a big gaping hole in it and it looked right into this convent. I used to tell the other kids that during the war an airplane crashed into it – to save face, y'know? 1981

In a certain way, the money aspect of it is not very useful to my parents. I gave them some money one day and found out later on that they didn't spend it. They thought that was going to be the pay off, you know; there wasn't gonna be any more. The whole thing of driving your folks up to some big house and saying, 'This is yours,' they don't want that. Then it's not them any more. 1981

I know my parents have a very deep love because they know and understand each other in a very realistic way. 1981

I wasn't brought up in a house where there was a lot of reading and stuff. I was brought up on TV. Who was William Burroughs? They never brought him up in high school in the Sixties – unless you hung around with that kind of crowd. And I didn't hang around with no crowd that was talking about William Burroughs. 1981

My father worked a whole lot of different places, worked in a rug mill for a while, drove a cab for a while, and he was a guard down at the jail for a while. I can remember when he worked down there, he used to always come home real pissed off, drunk, sat in the kitchen. 1981

At night, about nine o'clock, my father used to shut off the lights, every light in the house. And he used to get real pissed off if me or my sister turned any of them on. And he'd sit in the kitchen with a six pack and a cigarette. 1981

My mom, she'd set her hair and she would come downstairs and just turn on the TV and sit in the chair and watch TV till she fell asleep. And she'd get up the next morning and go to work again. 1981

In the summertime, when the weather got hot, I used to drag my mattress out of the window and sleep on the roof next door to the gas station. And I watched these different guys – the station closed at one and these guys, they'd be pulling and pulling out all night long. They'd be

meeting people there. They'd be ripping off down the highway. 1981

My mother, she's more sensitive. She thinks I should be an author. But I wanted to play guitar. So my mother, she's very Italian, she says 'This is a big thing, you should go see the priest'. 1981

Yeah, I like friends, but I'm pretty much by myself out there most of the time. My father was always like that. I lived with my father 20 years and never once saw a friend come over to the house. Not one time. 1981

As soon as I got 16, me and my buddy, we got this car and we started taking off. We used to take off down to the beach, sleep on top of beach houses. We used to spin up to the city, just walk around the streets all night long until the cops would catch us. 1981

I didn't even make it to class clown. I had nowhere near that amount of notoriety. I didn't have the flair to be a complete jerk. It was like I didn't exist. It was the wall, then me. But I was working on the inside all the time. A lot of rock'n'roll people went through this solitary experience. 1981

I know what it's like not to be able to do what you want to do, because when I go home that's what I see. It's no fun. It's no joke. I see my sister and her husband. They're living the lives of my parents in a certain kind of way. They got kids, they're working hard. They're just real nice, real soulful people. These are people you can see something in their eyes. It's really something. I know a lot of people back there. 1982

I lived 18 years of my life in a small town in New Jersey, next door to a gas station – Ducky Slattery's Sinclair Station. That was the guy's name, Ducky Slattery. He was an older guy and I lived next door. 1982

I asked my sister, 'What do you do for fun?' 'I don't have any fun,' she says. She wasn't kidding. 1982

They gave me the (draft) forms and I checked everything. Even said I was a homo and all that. Then this guy calls me into his office, talks to me for about three minutes and tells me to go home. 1982

When I was growing up, I lived in Freehold, New Jersey. My house had a front porch that overlooked this big tomato field across the street. I always used to go over there and have tomato fights – they were great. 1983

When I was growing up, there were two things that were unpopular in my house. One was me and the other was my guitar. We had this grate, like the heat was supposed to come through, except it wasn't hooked up to any of the heating ducts; it was just open straight down to the kitchen, and there was a gas stove right underneath it. When I used to start playing, my pop used to turn on the gas jets and try to smoke me out of the room. And I had to go hide out on the roof or something. 1983

Freehold was just a small town, a small, narrow-minded town, no different than probably any other provincial town. It was the kind of area where it was very conservative. It was just very stagnating. There were some factories, some farms and stuff, that if you didn't go to college, you ended up in. There really wasn't much, you know, there wasn't that much. 1984

He (Springsteen's father, photographed in his soldier's uniform after the end of the Second World War) looked like John Garfield in this great suit, he looked like he was going to eat the photographer's head off. I couldn't ever remember him looking that defiant or proud when I was growing up. I used to wonder what happened to all that pride, how it turned into so much bitterness. 1984

What I am doing today is directly connected to my mother. 1984

He had been so disappointed (his father), had so much stuff beaten out of him... that he couldn't accept the idea that I had a dream and I had

 BRUCE SPRINGSTEEN
IN HIS OWN WORDS

possibilities. The things I wanted, he thought were just foolish. 1984

Freehold was a real classic little town, very intent on maintaining the status quo. Everything was looked at as a threat. Kids were looked at as a nuisance and a threat. 1984

When I was growing up me and my dad used to go at it all the time over almost anything. I used to have really long hair, way down past my shoulders. I was 17 or 18, oh man, he used to hate it. We got to where we were fighting so much that I spent a lot of time out of the house. 1986

In the winter I remember standing downtown where it gets so cold and when the wind would blow I had this phone booth that I used to stand in and I used to call my girl for, like, hours at a time. 1986

I'd stand there in the doorway and, my dad, he'd be waiting for me in the kitchen and I'd tuck my hair down into my collar. I'd walk in and he'd call me back to sit down with him and the first thing he'd always ask me was what did I think I was doing with myself. And the worst part about it was that I could never explain to him. 1986

I remember I got in a motor-cycle accident once and I was laid up in bed. My dad had a barber come in and cut my hair and I can remember telling my dad I hated him and I would never, ever forget it. 1986

My dad used to tell me, 'I can't wait till the army gets you. When the army gets you they're gonna make a man out of you. They're gonna cut all that hair off and they'll make a man of you,' – this was, I guess, 1968. 1986

I remember the day I got my draft notice. I hid it from my folks and three days before my physical me and my friends went out and we stayed up all night and we got on the bus to go that morning and we were all so scared. Then I went and failed. I came home and after three days I walked into the kitchen and my mother and father were sitting there and they said, 'Where you been?' I said I took my physical. They said, 'What happened?' I said I failed and they said, 'That's good.' 1986

I remember when I was a kid. The first thing I remember is the living room of my grandparents' house where we lived. My grandfather had this big stuffed chair that he used to sit next to a kerosene stove. And I'd come running home from school and sit in that living room and I remember how safe I felt. 1987

Me and my first band were out in the middle of the country somewhere when we first went out on the road. We were broke and didn't have much money to get back. I remember calling my mom up and she said those magic words, 'You can always come home.' 1987

Leaving New Jersey

I lived in New Jersey for a very long time and
I've written a lot of things very tied into my past.
There's always different ghosts that you're
chasing and I felt that whatever they were, that
was done for me. I'd taken it as far as I could. I
was interested in making a break from whatever
people's perceptions of me were up to that point.
In my own life I was interested in putting some
distance between me and New Jersey, not New
Jersey the State, but part of whatever that meant
for me inside, and Los Angeles is a good place
to do this. I got a beautiful place, Patti and I got
together and babies and it was just a good place
where you have a lot of anonymity. The people
always came West to kinda re-find themselves or
recreate themselves in some fashion. This is the
town of recreation – mostly in some distorted
way – but it's just what you make it. 1992

STARTING OUT

*People used to tell me
that to be a success
I should say I was
from New York City.*
1973

I had all this stuff stored up for years, because there was no outlet in the bars I had been playing. No one's listening in a bar, and if they are, you've got a low PA system and they can't hear the words anyway. 1974

I listened to The Yardbirds' first two albums. And The Zombies, all those groups. And Them. 1974

THEM, FEATURING VAN MORRISON.

THE ZOMBIES.

THE YARDBIRDS, FEATURING ERIC CLAPTON.

I've got some great musicians in my band and I'm paying them terrible money. I pay myself the same, but it's terrible for me too. I mean, we're barely making a living scraping by. 1975

I was loving every minute of it, no matter what happened. I was NOT working, I was 20 years old, and I was running around loose, doing what I wanted to do. And I thought I was good. I didn't know if I was going to make it, I thought maybe I would not. Because you can never read these things out. 1977

My main thing was that it shouldn't feel like work. When I was a kid playing guitar, what I was trying to figure out was how to avoid work. So I worked it out, and when it started to get a little too much like work, my immediate impulse was to go away and go have fun, you know? But I guess it's got to be like that sometimes. 1977

They wouldn't let me in the bars because I wouldn't play Top 40. You should know the New Jersey shore bars, the people who smile at me today who wouldn't let me in the places then. It's true. Number one, they said I drew a bad crowd, an undesirable crowd. It wasn't a physically violent crowd, it was just kids, kids like me. But they didn't dig the kids. 1977

I was dead until I was 13. I didn't have any way of getting my feelings out. Then I found this thing. I was a drummer, but I wasn't working enough to buy a set of drums. So I bought a guitar. 1978

All these guys used to surf every day. I was friends with them all but never went. Finally, they got me. One afternoon they were merciless. They just kept taunting me and kidding me about not surfing that it just sort of got me riled. I grabbed a board and we all headed out to the beach. I must have been some sight surfing for the first time but I'll tell you something – I got the hang of it pretty quick. 1978

We used to play the Elks Club, the Rollerdome and the local insane asylum. One time this guy in a suit got up and introduced us for 20 minutes saying we were greater than The Beatles. Then the doctors came up and took him away. 1978

BRUCE, WITH CLARENCE CLEMONS ON SAXOPHONE.

It was never a down. Me and Steve (van Zandt) would always sit back and say, 'As bad as this is now, it will never be as bad as it was before we made an album or got a break'. 1978

My first guitar was one of the most beautiful sights I'd ever seen in my life. It was a magic scene. There it is: The Guitar. It was real and it stood for something: 'Now you're real'. I had found a way to do everything I wanted to do. 1978

The main reason I started doing my own arrangements and writing my own songs was because I hated to pick them up off the records. I didn't have the patience to sit down and listen to them, figure out the notes and stuff. 1978

I tried to live in California for a very short time but I soon found out the place held nothing for me. Musically I preferred what was going on in New Jersey. I didn't need to get a job because I could make money playing in the clubs. 1978

We wanted to play because we wanted to meet girls, make a ton of dough and change the world a little bit. 1980

I come from an area where there was not a lot of success. I don't know anyone who made a record before me. I didn't know anybody who had made anything. 1980

Even my mother when I told her I had a recording contract, said 'What'll you call yourself now?' But who you are, it's obvious isn't it? The one thing I learned is to be real. 1980

I never got into being discouraged because I never got into hoping. When I was a kid, I never got used to expecting success. I got used to failing. Once you do that, the rest is real easy. It took a lot of the pressure off. I just said, 'Hell, I'm a loser. I don't have to worry about anything'. I assumed immediately that nothing was happening. But that's not the same as giving up. You keep trying, but you don't count on things. 1980

The best thing that ever happened to me was when I got thrown out of the first band I was in and I went home and put on 'It's All Over Now' by The Rolling Stones and I learned that guitar solo. 1981

I think when I first started, I wouldn't allow myself to think that someday… I just wanted to get in a halfway band, be able to play weekends somewhere and make a little extra dough, working at some job during the week or something. Which is what my parents used to say that I could do. That was allowed. 1981

It was an easy life, just playing the bars. I had an emotional outlet. I wasn't exactly satisfied but I generally felt good about what I was doing even though it was no way big time stuff. I didn't know anybody who had made a record! Nobody I knew had anything too much. I mean, I didn't know anyone who'd even been as far as Pennsylvania! 1981

Some of those club owners were crazy. There was one guy, pulled out a gun one night and shot an amplifier. Can you see it? Smoke curling up to the ceiling. Absolutely quiet. And he says, 'I told you guys to turn it down'. 1982

BRUCE, WITH CHUCK BERRY.

Nobody would book us (early 1970s) because we never did any Top 40. Never. We used to play all old soul stuff, Chuck Berry, just the things we liked. That's why we couldn't get booked. We made enough to eat, though. 1982

I went into a state of shock as soon as I walked in (to the audition at CBS). Then Mike (Appel, his manager at the time) starts screaming and yelling about me – before I even played a note,

the hype began. I'm shrivelling up and thinking, 'Mike, please give me a break. Let me play a damn song'. 1982

Surfing was the only thing besides cars and music that I could relate to at that time (1969). 1982

When I was 18 and playing in this bar in California people would come up to us and say, 'Hey I really dig you guys! Where ya from?' And I'd say New Jersey and they'd just go, 'Yech! Ech!' 1982

I'd never been out of New Jersey in my life. Suddenly, I get to Esalen (the town in California where one of his early bands, Steel Mill, made their first appearance in the State) and see all these people walking around in sheets. I see some guys playing bongos in the woods. It turns out to be this guy who grew up around the corner from me. 1982

Somebody would take a solo and we'd all fall around laughing. The group (Dr. Zoom and the Sonic Boom, an ad hoc band with whom Springsteen played three concerts) had a Monopoly table set up in the middle of the stage. This was to give the people who didn't play anything a chance to be in the band. You know, so they could say, 'Yeah, I'm in Dr. Zoom. I play Monopoly'. 1982

The whole thing of… when I was 15 I wanted to play the guitar, I wanted to have a band, I wanted to travel. I wanted to be good, as good as I could be at the job. I was interested in being good at something that I felt was useful to other people, and to myself. 1984

When I started I just wanted to play rhythm guitar. Just stand back and play rhythm; no singing or anything. But I found out I knew a little more than I thought… more than the other guys that were in the band (The Castiles). 1984

I was the guy with a lot of energy and I would just look for places to put it. 1987

ROCK'N'ROLL

Rock'n'roll is my life's blood. Nothing means as much to me or ever has. I used to be crazy about a girl, walk 60 miles to her house, and sit in front of her house for hours. I don't really do that stuff any more, and I can't tell anyone that they're the most important thing in my life, because nothing in my life could ever be as important as this.
1977

Rock'n'roll, man, it changed my life. It was like The Voice of America, the real America coming into your home. It was the liberating thing, the out. Once I found the guitar, I had the key to the highway. 1978

When I was a kid what mattered to me more than the performance was the power of the music. People emphasise the personal too much. Being a rock star, that's the booby prize. Me, I set out to be a rock'n'roller. 1978

When I was growing up, the only thing that never let me down was rock'n'roll. Like rock'n'roll came to my house when there seemed no way out. It just seemed like a dead-end street. It reached down into all those homes where there was no music or books or any kind of creative sense and it infiltrated the whole thing. That's what happened in my house. 1981

Rock'n'roll is a means of erasing the past. You have to want to get away from something pretty bad. I wanted to perform. I wanted to travel. I wanted to feel free. 1981

Rock'n'roll's never about giving up. For me – for a lot of kids – it was a total positive force, not optimistic all the time, but positive. It was never, never, about surrender. 1981

God, so many kids seem to want to just completely lose themselves in rock. It's like escapism. Now, rock'n'roll gave me the chance to escape when I was a kid. When I listened to 'When My Little Girl Is Smiling' by The Drifters just the other day it reminded me all over again. 1981

But there are real things in this music – real emotions, real joy, real passion, hope – that I

BRUCE, WITH ROY ORBISON.

know are out there, right. Rock'n'roll gave me that sense of wonderment and it provided both the dream and a direct channel through which I could fulfil that dream. 1981

My whole life I was always around a lot of people whose lives just consisted of this compromising. They knew no other way – that's where rock'n'roll became important because it said there could be. 1981

Until I realised that rock music was my connection to the rest of the human race, I felt like I was dying, for some reason, and I didn't really know why. 1984

Rock'n'roll has been everything to me. The first day I can remember looking into a mirror and being able to stand what I saw was the day I had a guitar in my hand. 1984

I just know that when I started to play, it was like a gift. I started to feel alive. It was like some little guy stumbling down the street and finding

a key. Rock'n'roll was the only thing I ever liked about myself. 1984

Before rock'n'roll, I didn't have any purpose. I tried to play football and baseball and all those things and I just didn't fit. I was running through a maze. It was never a hobby. It was a reason to live. It was the only one I had. It was kind of life or death. 1985

If you grew up in my generation part of the dream of rock'n'roll was eternal youth, the endless Saturday night. 1987

I don't know about the question of what rock'n'roll means to anyone. I think every individual has got to answer that question for themselves at this point. I don't think there was ever anyone with an answer. It's like the difference between Jerry Lee Lewis and Elvis. At the time, they were both great. It's just that you've got to take it for what it is and see if you can make something out of it. 1987

SONGWRITING
& RECORDING

I just sit down and fuck around for a couple of hours. Usually something comes up. I sit down and I work on the song, and I sit down and work on it some more, then some more and some more.
1975

Last winter I wrote like a madman. Put it out. Had no money, nowhere to go, nothing to do. Didn't know too many people. It was cold and I wrote a lot. And I got to feeling very guilty if I didn't. Terrible guilt feelings. Like it was masturbation. That bad! 1972

I have the discipline to make myself write. I used to write every day on the buses, on the streets, but I tend to be more critical now, that's why I haven't written much recently. 1974

The mistake is to start thinking that you are your songs. To me a song is a vision, a flash: I see characters and situations. 1974

There's a lot of activity in my songs, a whole mess of people. It's like if you're walking down the street, that's what you see, but a lot of the songs were written without any music at all – it's just that I do like to sing the words! 1974

I work a lot on the lyrics before we record a song. I get self conscious about them. So I change them. It's the same with a lot of the old songs. I notice them, so even on some of the old songs I add new bits. 1974

The writing is more difficult now. On this album ('Born To Run'), I started slowly to find out who I am and where I wanted to be. It was like coming out of the shadows of various influences and trying to be me. You have to let more out of yourself all the time. You strip off the first layer, then the second, then the third. It gets harder because it gets more personal. 1975

All I do, like, I write down my impressions of stuff, like, and what I see, you know. 1975

I was fighting myself all the time, you know. Always do that. Everybody's hard on themselves; well, I take it to an extreme sometimes, where it starts like being self-defeating. In a way it's good because I think in the end you do pull out the best stuff, but it's really a mind-breaking project. It'll freak you out. You get frustrated and you go nuts. 1975

I ain't one of those guys who feels guilty if he didn't write something today. That's all jive. If I didn't do nothing all day, I feel great. 1976

You look around, you see people in the street dug in. You know they're already six feet under, people with nothing to lose and full of poison. I try to write about the other choice they've got. 1978

There comes a point where the song becomes more and more like a movie. And when that happens you cease to become its creator and assume the role of director. For you have to be so many different characters and it's better to let them have lives of their own. 1978

It should be dance music. It's a very alive feeling I try to get into the songs – no matter what the situation. The people in the songs are alive. 1980

I go onstage and feel myself. And I'm not worrying about 'Oh man that note sounds like this dude. Hey man, I heard that word off of 'Subterranean Homesick Blues'. At one time it worried me but it doesn't any more, because when I get onstage finally I feel myself. That's who I am. 1980

The songs I write, they don't have particular beginnings and they don't have endings. The camera focuses in and then out. 1980

The details in the songs are always secondary, which doesn't mean they aren't important to get right. But detail alone is just detail. I have a lot of songs sitting in my notebook that are full of detail, but missing the emotion which ties the whole thing together and breathes life into it. 1981

I'm not writing for the people I grew up with as a kid because they're all married with a dog and kids now. 1981

I don't know how important the settings are in the first place. It could be New Jersey, it could be California, it could be Alaska. The

images are like the colouring, not necessarily
the picture. I can float anywhere – uptown,
downtown, anywhere. I want to do everything. I
want to see everything. I want to go everywhere.
1982

The point in a lot of my stuff is that they're like
scenarios, they're like plays. And the power is
not so much in the immediate imagery or the
immediate physical picture that's presented, as
it is in a certain battle being waged between
just whatever forces are in the songs. So
generally, I write things on a bigger-than-life
scale in a certain way. 1982

The subject I sing about is not necessarily what I
sing about. I'll use situations and probe for the
very basic emotions. The conflicts I sing about
are present in every level of life from the street
level to the business level. 1982

I write about moments. I don't write about
the every day. I write a lot about action
moments, moments when people are pushed to
take a certain action, to do something, to do
anything to get out of their present situation
or circumstances or predicament – to step out,
to get out of that boring thing, to break loose.
1982

I usually don't teach the band the songs until
we are in the studio, until we're about to
record. Then I show them the chords real quick
so they can't learn how to play it, because the
minute they learn how to play it, they start
figuring out the parts and they get self
conscious. The first two takes, when they're just
learning it, they're worried about hanging on.
So they're playing really tight at the edge and
they're playing very intuitively which is, in
general, how our best stuff happens right now.
1984

To try and control a record is to just try and
limit it. It's the same thing with a child. A kid.
Once he gets to a certain point, it's his own life
and you gotta give him room. And it's the same
thing, I guess, with music or probably any type
of creation or creative thing. 1984

The main thing with my songs right now is that I write them to be complete things. They're filled with a lot of geographical detail and a lot of detail about what people are wearing, where they live. 1984

I don't know what I'm writing from, but the main thing I've always been worried about was me. I had to write about me all the time, every song, because in a way, you're trying to find out what that 'me' is. That's why I chose where I grew up, and where I live, and I take situations I'm in, and people I know, and take them to the limits. 1984

Part of the thing is that when I write a song, I write it to be a movie – not to make a movie, to be a movie, like 'Highway Patrolman' or 'Racing In The Street'. It's only six minutes. You could really screw it up in an hour and a half. 1984

You write the song just for yourself, but it's no good unless you play it for somebody else. That's the connection between people that is forever lasting and can never be broken apart. 1985

It's like those Italian Westerns at the drive-in. I always loved it that they showed them all at once. That's the way I make these albums – so they all get played at once. 1985

I wanted to write songs I can get up and sing without feeling embarrassed. I have tried to write to my age along the way. 1987

I have a lot of desire to control my output, to control what's coming out. Writing a good song is never easy but it's not as pained and I don't put myself through a lot of extraneous bull like I used to 10 years ago. 1987

The only trick to writing a new song is you have to have a new idea. And to have a new idea, you've got to be a bit of a new person, so that's where the challenge is. 1987

I suppose the love song has tended to be romantic in a bit of a one-dimensional way. Not everyone's Elvis Costello and has written tremendous love songs. I thought that if I was going to write this kind of music it should be three-dimensional or multi-dimensional. 1987

LIVE

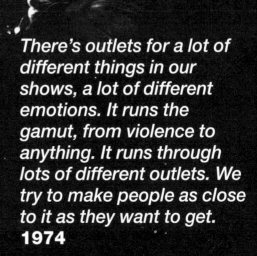

There's outlets for a lot of different things in our shows, a lot of different emotions. It runs the gamut, from violence to anything. It runs through lots of different outlets. We try to make people as close to it as they want to get.
1974

I mean, you play all the time half sick but it got to the point where I couldn't play piano, I was spitting blood. I don't get sick a whole lot but this year we have been. We've done so many gigs this past year that it just starts to collect… the fatigue. 1974

Usually we won't play any place over 3,000 – that's the highest we want to do. We don't want to get any bigger. And that's even too big. I'm always disappointed in acts that go out and play those places. I don't know how the band can go out and play like that. I don't know how Joni Mitchell can do it. You can't. You can't effectively do it. 1974

All I know is that those big coliseums ain't where it's supposed to be. There's always something else going on all over the room. You go to the back row, you can't see the stage, talk about what's on it. You see a blot of light. You better bring your binocs… especially our band – it would be impossible to reach out there the way we try to do. Forget it! 1974

Every time you get on stage, you have to prove something. It doesn't matter if they've heard you or not. The kid on the street will make up his own mind. The music is what really matters. That's the way it has always been. 1975

We had the problem of any opening act (on their early tour supporting Chicago) playing in 20,000 seat halls. They just won't listen to you. They can't hear, for one thing. They don't know how to listen, for another. Some groups just go out and plough through it. But I can't do it that way. And it showed – I did 13 or 14 gigs in them big halls and we sold no records. 1975

I think, for most musicians, it has to be like life or death or else it's not worth it. That's why every night we play a real long time, and we play real hard. I want to be able to go home and say I went all the way tonight – and then I went a little further. 1978

It's a little easier to lead the band without the guitar. You can get a little better picture of what you're going for. 1978

I'm always jumping into the audience, when they're not jumping into me. 1978

See, we originally started off with a two hour set. But when the tour got underway we found it impossible to keep it down to that. It was hard for me to leave anything out. So now I play as long as it feels right. Some nights it's too long and others it ain't long enough. I guess most of the songs are pretty durable, at least, from the reaction they still get, they seem to be. 1978

See, it's their night. You may get sore, you may get hoarse, but when you see all those kids out there it's like the first show all over again. 1981

What happens is that a lot of the security in a lot of places don't understand. Kids get real excited, but they're not mean, they're just excited. 1980

I get excited staying at all those different hotels, in a whole lot of rooms. Home never has a big attraction for me. I'm always curious what the wallpaper's gonna be like. Do I have a big bed or a little one? And what's this funny painting? 1980

My whole thing when playing live is to do it with a sense of inner self-confidence. I have to feel in control. Instinctively, it's got to feel right because when I play live my music has nothing to do with feeling relaxed. That's a key difference: it's more the challenge, it's about delivering everything you've got. 1981

I'm on stage for three hours and every muscle in my body is, like, tight for that three hours. I feel like I got a stick up my back. 1981

If I leave the stage feeling, 'Well, if I played just one more song, maybe somebody out there would be won over'. If I feel I could have given more, it's hard for me to sleep that night. 1981

The shows aren't a casual thing, even though they are filled with fun and wildness. There should be beauty, but there's also got to be ugliness and brutality. If you don't have all of that in the evening, you're not doing it. If you

turn away, that's the beginning of the end. That's what you spend your time doing – trying not to turn away. 1985

I'm real lucky. I get to have a little bit of my dream every night. 1985

I'm out there doing something at night that I can never get from anything else. I guess I feel most at home on stage. 1985

Some nights when I'm up there, I feel like the king of the world. It's the greatest feeling on earth. I can go home and get in bed and sleep real sound. It's a beautiful thing. Beautiful. It can tune you into everything, what's happening with people everywhere. 1985

Among those 100 (fans) there's at least one for whom you're a hero. He saved money to see you. That's what I did, I played for that guy. 1987

If you get a good band and play your stuff real well and present it in a clear and concise fashion – and the audience is receptive, which the audiences have been – then you can do whatever you want to do. 1987

BRUCE AND CLARENCE CLEMONS STRIKE A POSE DURING THE TRIUMPHANT BORN IN THE USA TOUR.

After the shows I usually go home and eat my dinner at 2 a.m. and sometimes I go out and take a walk; there is nowhere open. I like to go out in the city at night, it's quiet and nice in the summertime. I come back and sometimes I read or play some music and get some sleep. 1987

The show just evolved out of the club act. Right up to the 'Born To Run' tour basically people were standing where they had been standing for 14 years. When we first started rehearsing I said to the equipment guys, 'Put everybody's stuff on the other side of the stage, switch everything around'. It was funny, we couldn't do it. 1987

What I do is I try to put different elements together, I want them to interact differently. With old friends that is important. 1987

A lot of it is about being there which is why we haven't done much television or the video thing which allows too much distance. Our band is about breaking down distance. 1987

A good night out, that's basically what this is all about. They can come to put aside their worries for a minute maybe, enjoy themselves, dance, a little bit of a sing-a-long. I try to present a lot of different things so it can be something that challenges or changes the way you think about something – your life, your job, your friends. We try to supply what ever they may need at that moment, some inspiration maybe. 1987

Playing big arenas is not that different. It just means being mentally aware of the audience. It is not that different from playing a theatre. The crowd is very important to the show. I like playing stadiums quite a lot. 1987

We got so many songs that are fun to play. There is a lot of room for having a good time. 1987

I just started to talk to people (during concerts) because it seemed like a normal thing to do. I always see the audience as a person. I imagine that I am talking to them one-to-one. It is why I picked the guitar up. The talking is just something that kind of came up. 1987

My job is to blow into town and tell everybody to keep going, and blow on out. 1987

FANS

You don't go out there to deliver $47.50 worth of music. My whole thing is to go out there and deliver what they could not possibly buy.
1978

Everything counts. Every person, every individual in the crowd counts to me. I see it both ways. There is a crowd reaction. But then I also think very, very personally, one to one with the kids. Because you put out the effort and then if it doesn't come through it's a breakdown. What I always feel is that I don't like to let people that have supported me down. 1978

I've had kids writing me letters saying, 'I saw you and you changed the way I thought about this' or, 'You changed my life'. I think you do have an effect – anything that inspires anyone on any level to take any kind of positive action, that's what I want. Even if it's only for one night. 1978

You can't conform to the formula of always giving the audience what it wants or you're killing yourself and you're killing the audience. Just because they respond to something doesn't mean they want it. I think it has come to the point where they respond automatically to things they think they should respond to. You've got to give them more than that. 1975

See, I'm not into people screaming at me, like Bowie. Once they do that, it's over. I'll go back to playing the small clubs. I'm not there for them anyway. I'm there for me, you know. If they can dig it, cool, if not, they don't have to come. 1976

When I grew up, rock and roll was the only thing that was ever true, and it was the only thing that never let me down. You've got a lot to live up to when you walk out on that stage – a certain tradition from the early rockers up; to know that I believe in a lot. It's like, you've got to be your own hero, find it for yourself. 1978

The greatest thing is going backstage after the show and seeing some kid there, not screwed up on drugs, but someone whose face is all lit up. It's like you've done something to get things stirred up inside his head. That's the whole idea – get excited, do something… be your own hero. 1978

For the first four years I had an attitude. I went into every place expecting it to be empty. So whoever was there was a big plus. I was glad they were there, and we played our best to whoever was there, always. You just don't lie back in this band, you know. That just don't happen. That's why people come down to see us – because something more is going to happen. Something – just somehow, some way. 1978

It's funny. At the start of the shows the girls would jump on stage, then, after realising what they had done, just stand there and freeze. But now they're getting used to it – and so are their tongues! 1978

They even come around to my house and wait for hours outside. I got a kid sister back in San Francisco and when she tells her friends who her brother is they go wild. Ain't it just amazing? 1978

That's what I thought about in the studio. I thought about going out and meeting people I don't know. Going to France and Germany and Japan and meeting Japanese people and French people and German people, meeting them and seeing what they think, and being able to go over there with something. To go over there with a pocketful of ideas or to go over there with just something, to be able to take something over. And boom! To do it! 1980

I guess you just don't want to let them down. You want to show people that somehow

somewhere somebody can do it. Mainly, it's important to have the passion for living. 1980

I think the one feeling that's most unique to this job, the best part of the whole thing, is meeting someone like this guy the other night who had been on a bus 10 hours. He's 21 years old and he just grabs hold of me. We're in a room crowded with people. He's crying and he doesn't care. He says, 'It's my birthday', and I ask, 'How are old you?' He says, 'I'm 21, and this is the most important thing in my life'. And you know they're not kidding when they say it, because you look in their faces and they're so full of emotion. 1981

You meet somebody, and it's like an open well. In 10 minutes you'll know more about him than his mother and father do, and maybe his best friend. 1981

I think that one of the problems is that the audience and the performer have got to leave some room for each other to be human, or else they don't really deserve each other, in a funny kind of way. 1984

My audience, I hope, would be all sorts of people, rich and poor, middle class people, I don't feel like I'm singing towards any one group of people. I don't want to put up those kinds of walls, that's not really what our band is about. 1984

The idealising of performers or politicians doesn't seem to make much sense. It's based on an image and an image is always basically

limiting and only a portion, and only the public's portion of that individual's personality. Which is not to say that it is false, but it's not complete. 1984

The biggest gift that your fans can give you is just treating you like a human being, because anything else dehumanizes you. And that's one of the things that has shortened the life spans, both physically and creatively, of some of the best rock'n'roll musicians – that cruel isolation. If the price of fame is that you have to be isolated from the people you write for, then that's too fucking high a price to pay. 1984

I feel the night you look into your audience and you don't see yourself, and the night the audience looks at you and they don't see themselves, that's when it's all over. 1984

While you do have the responsibility to do a good job, you don't have a responsibility of carrying 20,000 people's dreams and desires. That's their jobs. 1985

There are unreasonable demands made upon you in this business, and at the same time there are unreasonable rewards. You get a tremendous amount of people's affection, sincere affection. 1985

You want people to see that you are a human being, and you are doing your best under difficult circumstances like everybody is. That's one of the things you want to communicate, 'Hey, it's tough, but keep going'. 1985

When I go on stage, my approach is 'I'm going to reach just one person' – even if there's 80,000 people there. Maybe those odds aren't so great, but if that's what they are, that's okay. 1987

I want my audience to respond to me basically as a person, as a human being. 1987

You may be playing 80 shows in eight months, but this kid out there, it's his money, and it's his one night. He may not see you again for a year. So you mustn't let him down. 1987

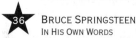

SONGS

It was just like my heart spoke straight through my mouth (on 'Dancing In The Dark'), without even having to pass through my brain.
1987

BRUCE, WITH CRYSTAL TALIEFERO, DURING THE 1992 HUMAN TOUCH TOUR.

I thought it was important to do that song ('New York Serenade'). It completes the set for me. It might get more response to do a boom-boom thing and really rock the joint. But when I walked down the steps afterwards I felt complete. Otherwise, I might have messed up. 1975

I wanted 'Born To Run' to be a hit single. Not for the bucks but because I really believed in the song a whole lot and I just wanted to hear it on the radio, on AM across the country. For me, that's where a song should be. 1975

'Born To Run' was about New York. I was there for months. I had this girl with me and she'd just come in from Texas and she wanted to go home again and she was going nuts and we were in this room and it just went on and on. I'd come home practically in tears. And I was sort of into that whole thing of being nowhere. But knowing there is something someplace. 1975

I don't write songs about lawsuits. 'The Promise' is rather about the price everyone pays for success – and the dangers settling for anything less. 1977

Oh sure, some of the characters on a track like, say, 'Rosilita' are people I've come across in my life. But most of my songs are fantasies. Should a song reflect imagery of the performer as he really is? You can't get away from the fact that you are making the statements, but then again, is it the song that does that? 1978

I think that all the great records and great songs say, 'Hey, take this and find your place in the world. Do something with it, do anything with it. Find some place to make your stand, no matter how big or small it is'. That's a pretty wonderful thing for a record to do. 1981

I love those Beach Boys songs. I love 'Don't Worry Baby'. If I hear that thing in the right mood, forget it. I go over the edge, you know? But I said, 'How do you feel right now?' So I write 'Racing In The Street' and that felt good. 1985

It's not that people aren't taught to think, but that they're not taught to think hard enough. 'Born In The USA' is not ambiguous. All you got to do is listen to the verses. If you don't listen to the verses, you're not gonna get the whole song, you're just gonna get the chorus. What you do if someone doesn't understand your song is you keep singing it. 1987

If you've ever pushed a car down the street and felt like the biggest jerk in the world, this one's for you ('Used Cars'). 1987

You move on, you change. You're not the same person you were. You can't come out and play oldies, because then you're a damn oldies act. You can't come out and push people's buttons with old songs. It's a waste of time, a waste of my time and a waste of their time. I wasn't interested in coming out and being nostalgic, which you can do even after just one successful tour. 1987

The classic thing for me is the misinterpretation of 'Born In The USA'. I opened the paper one day and saw where they had quizzed kids on what different songs meant. 'Well, it's about my country,' they answered. Well, that is what it's about, but if that's as far in as you go, you're going to miss it, you know? I don't think people are being taught to think hard enough about things in general- whether it's about their own lives, politics, the situation in Nicaragua or whatever. 1987

'10th Avenue' is about having my band, having the guys around you, about letting rip a little bit. 1987

I wanted 'Jersey Girl' to feel like you're in a convertible and it's a summer night and you're driving real slow and you're driving in the town you grew up in but you're different, you've changed but something that is forever is driving with you. 1987

When I was sitting at home, thinking about coming on tour and trying to decide what I was going to do. I thought, well, I got to sing a new song. That's my job. But this is an old song which I wrote when I was 24 years old, sitting on the edge of my bed in Long Beach, New Jersey, and thinking, 'Here I come, world!' When I wrote it, I guess I figured it was a song about a guy and a girl who wanted to run and keep on running. But as I got older and as I sang it over the years, it sort of opened up, and I guessed I realised that it was about two people searching for something better... anyway, this song has kept me good company on my search. I hope it's kept you good company on your search (intro to 'Born To Run'). 1988

BRUCE AND THE E STREET BAND TAKE A BOW, LEFT TO RIGHT: CLARENCE CLEMONS, BRUCE, STEVE VAN ZANDT, DANNY FEDERICI, GARRY TALLENT, MAX WEINBERG AND ROY BITTAN.

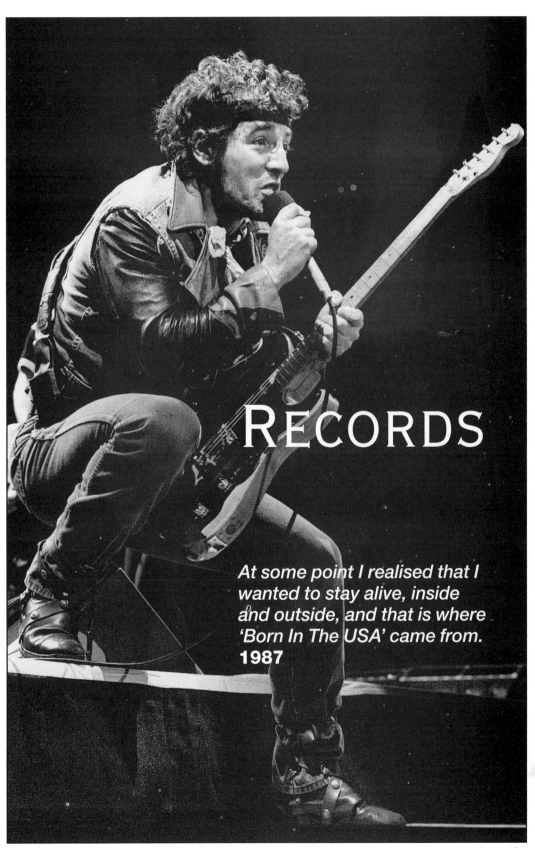

RECORDS

At some point I realised that I wanted to stay alive, inside and outside, and that is where 'Born In The USA' came from.
1987

they came from. A few of them I worked on for a week or so, but most of them were just jets, a real energy situation. 1974

I remember when I did my first record, I thought it was dynamite. I had a tremendous amount of confidence for some reason. Then I began to question my work really hard. I was no longer interested in what I was doing well, I was interested in what I wasn't doing well. I felt I was failing because part of the picture was missing. That began with the 'Darkness' record. 1985

'The Wild, The Innocent & The E Street Shuffle'

We were just sitting there, flashing on everything that was happening. I was exactly where I wanted to be. I had a band. I knew who I was. We were getting work. The album reflects that. 1980

On the second album, I started slowly to find out who I am and where I wanted to be. It was like coming out of the shadow of various influences and trying to be yourself. 1982

'Greetings From Asbury Park'

Like, the main reason I put Asbury Park on the title of the album was because they were pushing for this big New York thing, this big town. I said, 'Wait, you guys are nuts or something. I'm from Asbury Park, New Jersey. Can you dig it? New Jersey'. 1974

The summer I was doing the first album and the summer before that I spent a lot of time in Asbury. But all the heavy personal stuff in my songs comes from spending time further up the beach. 1974

I got a lot of things out in that first album. I let out an incredible amount at once – a million things in each song. They were written in half-hour, fifteen-minute blasts. I don't know where

'Born To Run'

It's not actually a concept type thing, but it's like you get a jigsaw puzzle and you put it down on the floor and it slowly comes together. 1975

It's going to feature songs around a feeling, a mood. It's going to need more instruments than the other albums to get that feel, but it can be done. 1975

Here comes the third album, and I guess everybody's excited about it. My time has come, but I'm not going to count on it. I don't count on nothing. I stopped doing that a long time ago. Anything that happens now is icing on the cake. 1975

I was unsure about 'Born To Run' all the way. I didn't really know what I put down on it. I lost all perspective. The sessions turned into something I never conceived of a record turning into. It turned into this thing that was wrecking me, just pounding me into the ground. Every time you'd win a little victory over it, accomplish a little something, you'd say, 'Well, the worst is over.' The next day you'd come back in and it would start pounding away at you again. 1978

I hated it. I couldn't stand to listen to it. I thought it was the worst piece of garbage I'd ever heard. I told Columbia I wouldn't release it. I told 'em I'd just go to the Bottom Line and do all the new songs and make it a live album. 1978

I had this horrible pressure in the studio, and for the whole last part of the record, I was living in this certain inn in New York over in the West Side. And the room there had this crooked mirror and every night when I'd come home, that mirror was crooked again. Every time. That crooked mirror, it just couldn't stay straight. 1978

The best thing you can say about the album is that it was the most intense experience I ever had. There was nothing ever came close. And what was worse was, like if you can imagine being at the particular height of intensity for, like, four months. Some days when you got in there it was like murder. Some of the stuff that was in the air in that studio was deadly. People would back off. 1978

The only concept that was around 'Born To Run' was that I wanted to make a big record, you know, that sounds like these words. Just like a car, zoom, straight ahead, that when the sucker comes on it's like wide open. No holds barred! 1978

I was going to have a song about back home on it, but I didn't get to it. There's a few oblique references but most of the songs are about being nowhere. 1978

One night, towards the end of the record, I was sitting there at the piano trying to get down the last cut, 'She's The One,' and Landau's in the booth, and we've been at it for hours and hours.

I just lean my head down on the piano. It just won't come. And everyone's trying to tell me how to do it and Landau's saying this and that and freaking out and, all of a sudden, everybody looks around and Landau has just disappeared, just walked off into the night – night, it was like six a.m. – couldn't take it. 1978

The album became a monster. It wanted everything. It just ate up everyone's life. 1978

It was the weirdest thing I have ever seen. We did attempt to work on it earlier. We did the song 'Born To Run' a year ago. And over that period, we did attempt to start the record many times. But we'd always get bogged down. Things broke. Sessions didn't work. 1978

The main factor that changed things round, I guess, was Jon Landau. He was an interested party. He said, 'Listen, man, you got to make an album'. Like he said, I wasn't doing right by myself putting the album off as long as I did. He sort of impressed on me this fact. 1978

It really dealt with faith and a searching for answers... I laid out a set of values. A set of ideas, intangibles like faith and hope, belief in friendship and in a better way. 1980

I was born, grew old and died making the album. 1980

My early albums were about being some place and what it was like there. 'Born To Run' is about being nowhere at all. 1980

It had a lot of overblown romance but it still contained the seeds of realism. 1981

The one thing that bothered me about the 'Born To Run' record was when it was initially criticised by people who thought it was a record about escape. To me, there was an aspect of that, but I always felt it was more about searching. 1984

On the old stuff, there's a lot of characters and groups of people and as it goes along it thins out; people drop by the wayside, until on 'Born To Run', it's essentially two: it's a girl and a guy. 1984

I was very doubtful of myself. You are just trying to find out about your feelings to a lot of things. 1987

At the end of the record I tended to look back at it and think, 'Well, it was good enough for now but these people have to go somewhere'. You just can't go, you can't go all the time. Basically, to have some meaning they had to be going some place. Where were these two people going? I didn't know myself. 1987

All my records were a reaction to 'Born To Run'. I asked all the questions on that album that I'm still asking today. You can't find it until you strip away the illusion. You gotta strip away the fairy tale. 1987

I wanted to make a record that would sound like Phil Spector. I wanted to write words like Dylan. I wanted my guitar to sound like Duane Eddy. 1987

When I was writing 'Born To Run' I was interested in writing bigger than life, bigger than lifesize. Lately, I've been trying to scale it down. 1987

When you hear 'Born To Run' it breathes with all the years that have passed. The audience have made a lot of my songs their own. It is as much their song as my song. 1987

The real question in 'Born To Run' which I asked is that I want to know if love is real. 1987

'Darkness On The Edge Of Town'

It was just an album about a lot of things in life and in the world for me, where you can see a lot in a lot of people's faces. They've had the humanity beaten out of them. You see the guys on the street that are just mad, they'll take a slug at anything, the guy with the crazy eyes... events just beat the humanity out of people till there's nothing left. 1978

It's a weird thing about those reviews. You can find any conceivable opinion in them. One guy says the record's exactly like 'Born To Run and it's great, the next one says it's not like 'Born To Run' and it's great, the next one says it's not like 'Born To Run' and it's awful. 1978

When I was making this particular album, I just had a specific thing in mind. And one of the important things was that it had to be just a relentless barrage of the particular thing. 1978

It's hard to explain without getting too heavy. What it is, it's the characters' commitment. In the face of all the betrayals, in the face of all the imperfections that surround you in whatever kind of life you lead, it's the characters' refusal to let go of their own humanity, to let go their own belief in the other side. It's a certain loss of innocence – more so than in the other albums. 1978

I was so blown away by what happened last time, I initially thought of doing no ads. Just put it out, literally just put it out. 1978

Most of the songs were written real fast. It was just figuring out what to do with them. 1978

This album's stripped down to run as clean as possible and stay true. 1978

The characters aren't kids. They're older – you been beat, you been hurt. But there's still hope, there's always hope. They throw dirt on you all your life, and some people get buried so deep in the dirt that they'll never get out. The album is about people who will never admit that they're buried that deep. 1978

I think it's less romantic – it's got more, a little more, isolation. It's sort of like I said, 'Well, listen, I'm 28 years old and the people in the album are around my age'. I perceive them to be that old and they don't know what to do. There's less a sense of a free ride than there is on 'Born To Run'. There's more a sense of: 'If you want to ride, you're going to pay. And you'd better keep riding'. 1978

For me the whole thing in 'Darkness' is just people stretching for the light in the darkness, just people trying to hold on to the things they believe in the face of the battering from the outside. 1978

The general tone of the album tells what it was like the last few years. It had me up; it had me down. When I was off, though, I never doubted. I never lost track of what I was trying to do. 1978

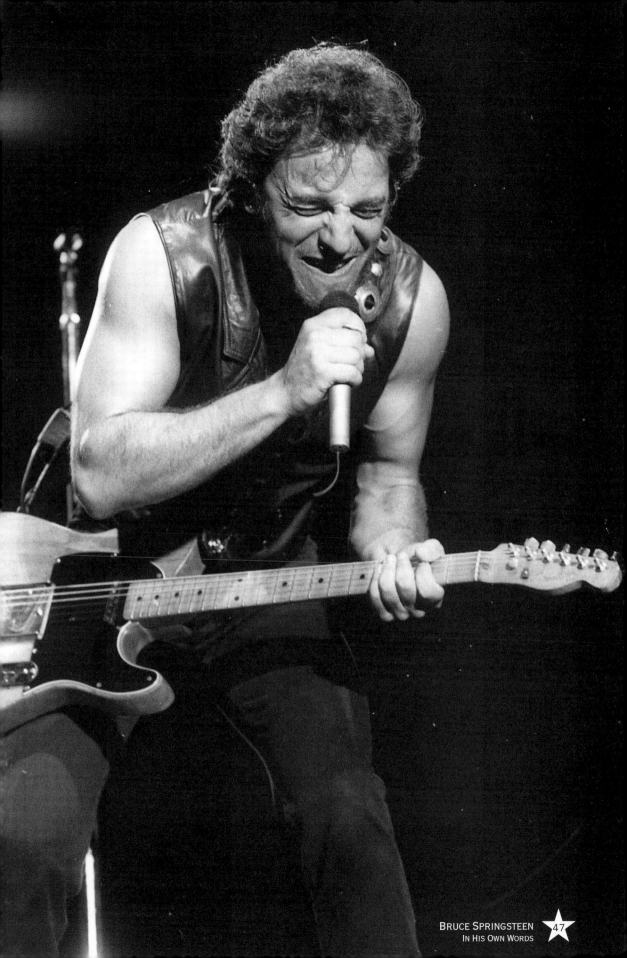

It's like everybody's always in transit. There's no settling down, no fixed action. You pick up the action, and then at some point – psst! – the camera pans away, and whatever happened, that's what happened. 1980

Rock'n'roll has always been this joy, this certain happiness that is in its way the most beautiful thing in life. But rock is also about hardness and coldness and being alone. With 'Darkness', it was hard for me to make those things coexist. How could a happy song like 'Sherry Darling' coexist with 'Darkness On The Edge of Town'? 1980

I had a big awakening in the past two, three years. Much bigger than people would think. Learned a lot of things, saw a lot of things. Realised a lot of things about my own past. So it's there on the record. I'm more alive than I ever was, and that is the story. 1978

It was about a guy stripping himself down, trying to find out where he stands. 1987

It was dry, recording wise. I felt that I over sang, we under played and over sang a little bit. It was rather different in performance. 1987

'The River'

On 'The River' I would tend to have songs that were kind of celebrations and darker songs next to each other. That was because I didn't know how to combine them. I didn't know how to synthesise it into one song. I knew it was all part of the same picture which is why 'The River' was a double album. 1984

It was about trying to get connected back with your relationships. It was the first record where people were married on it. 1987

I wasn't going to put 'Out In The Street' on the album because it's all idealism. It's about people being together and sharing a certain feeling. I know the feeling is real, but it's hard to see sometimes. You go out in the street and there's a chance you get hit over the head or mugged. The song's not realistic in a way, but there's something very real at the heart of it. 1981

'Nebraska'

The record was just basically about people being isolated from their jobs, from their friends, from their family, from their fathers, their mothers, not being connected to anything that's going on, your government. And I think when that happens, there's just a whole breakdown. When you lose that sense of the community, there's some spiritual breakdown that occurs. You just get shot off somewhere where nothing really matters. 1980

It was about a spiritual crisis in which man is lost. He's isolated from the government, isolated from his job. That happens in this country (USA), don't you see, all the time. It seems to be part of modern society. I don't know what anybody can do about it. 1980

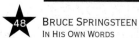

I was renting a house on this reservoir, and I didn't go out much, and for some reason I started to write. I was interested in writing smaller than I had been, writing with just detail. I guess my influences at that time were the movie (Terence Malick's Badlands) and these stories by Flannery O'Connor. 1981

A lot of its content was in its style, in the treatment of it. It needed that kind of austere, echoey sound, just the one guitar – one guy kinda telling his story. That was what made the record work – the conversational sound like you were just meeting people and they told you what either happened to them or what was happening to them. 1984

I had a certain tone in my mind which I felt was the tone of… it was funny because in a way it felt like the tone of what I felt like when I was a kid growing up, and at the same time it felt like the tone of what the country felt like to me at

that moment. That was the kind of heart I was drawing from. 1984

There were songs that didn't get on to 'Nebraska' because they didn't say anything in the end. They had no meaning. That's the trickiest thing to do and that was my only test of songs: Is this believable? Is this real? Do I know this person? 1984

I wanted to make it feel like you meet somebody. The 'Nebraska' stuff was like that. You meet somebody and you walk a little while in their shoes and see what their life is like. And then what does it mean to you? That's kind of the direction my writing is going in – it's just the thing I find most satisfying. Just saying what somebody had to say and not making too big a deal out of it. 1985

'Nebraska' was rock bottom. I came home from tour and I sat down for two months and I wrote

ON STAGE DURING AN LA BENEFIT CONCERT IN 1986, LEFT TO RIGHT: DANNY FEDERICI, STEPHEN STILLS, GRAHAM NASH, DAVID CROSBY, BRUCE, NEIL YOUNG AND NILS LOFGREN.

the whole thing. I recorded and mixed it in my bedroom and put it out on cassette. I always think of it as my most personal record. What happens when all the things you believe in when you are 25 don't work? What happens when all these things just break down? Your friends fail you, or you fail your friends. When you're alone – can you live? Can you go on? 1987

It was really well supported by my audience, which was real satisfying and in tune. So, I say, hey, let's do some things, get in there. I can't stand in one place. You've got to take some chances. 1987

'Born In The USA'

Mainly all my records try to offer some sort of survival course. Maybe you can't dream the same dreams when you're 34 that you did when you were 24, you know, but you can still dream something. Maybe you've got to

downsize some of your expectations. I know I have. Just in growing up, in accepting childhood. My characters, I think that's what they do. 1987

The guy in 'Born In The USA' wants to strip away that mythic America which was Reagan's image of America. He wants to find something real and connecting. He's looking for a home in his country. 1987

I think 'Born In The USA' kind of casts a suspicious eye on a lot of things. That's the idea. These are not the same people any more and it's not the same situation. These are survivors and I guess that's the bottom line. 1987

As I get older I write about me, I guess, and what I see happening around me and my family. So that's 'Born In The USA'. 1987

I wasn't satisfied with the 'Born In The USA' record. I did not think I made all the connections I wanted to make on it. 1987

'Bruce Springsteen & The E Street Band Live: 1975 – 1985'

We played the live album in my room. We all sat there and listened to it. And I said, 'Well 10 years, there it is. When you have those little babies and they want to know what you did these past 10 years, you play them this record'. I think it is something to be proud of. 1987

We all kind of sat there listening to it and sensed that it was the end of something and that next time would be different. 1987

It will have to sell on its own. It covers the years between 1975 and 1985 so that those who first discovered Springsteen with 'Born In The USA' will have an idea of what I did before. 1987

We had made tapes over the years but never used them. We recorded every tour. We settled on the idea of doing a record from different phases of the band – if you saw us in a club or in an arena. 1987

There was some songs that I like that we had to leave off. I would have liked 'Glory Days' on it but we had banged 72 minutes on each CD and that was the most you could get. 1987

'Tunnel Of Love'

I think the 'Tunnel Of Love' album just sort of happened on one hand, and, at the same time, I was interested in personalising my music. It's just a natural thing you have to do. You put something out there, it gets pulled in and taken up, and becomes part of the culture and part of people's lives. And then you have to reinvent yourself. I felt that made sense after 'Born In The USA'. 1987

'Tunnel Of Love' is basically stripped-down soul music. So, I just fleshed it out, put the horns in there and got in the mood of it. And it translates really easily, in a very relaxed fashion, to a big stage. 1987

As far as an album goes it is my best collection of songs to come out at one time. It was new stuff, stuff I'd not written about before, except sparsely. Usually there is a lot of conflict when I put my records out, but I was happy that this one came out. 1987

I wanted to write some love songs in a way that had not been done in exactly that way before. 1987

The record was made very quickly, in two or three weeks. It was a very peaceful working process and the record was intimate. I wanted the record to be non mythic, just real. Smaller's not the right word, not austere – clean, arranged. I worked six hours a day and the songs came pretty easy. I do not remember struggling. 1987

I wasn't trying to write a record which was bright or dark, to me the record is a friend. 1987

Hopefully, if you write a good record or make any good piece of art it's like a well where people can go to it for fun, sustenance, faith, companionship and they can speak to who they are now in their lives. That was the main thing I wanted the record to do. 1987

To me, the record had a certain doubt to it but I do not know anyone in a relationship who doesn't have that feeling or any of the feelings that are on the record. 1987

I wanted it to be anti-illusion. I wanted to write personally and that is what I do best. 1987

The main thing was to show people striving for that idea of home: people forced out of their homes, people looking for their homes, people trying to build their homes, people looking for shelter, for comfort, for tenderness, a little bit of kindness somewhere. 1988

I wanted to make a record about what I felt, about really letting another person in your life and trying to be part of someone else's life. That's a frightening thing, something that's always filled with shadows and doubts, and also wonderful and beautiful things. 1988

That sense of dread, man – it's everywhere. It's outside, it's inside, it's in the bedroom, it's on the street. 1988

It's difficult because there's a part of you that wants the stability and the home thing, and there's a part of you that isn't so sure. I couldn't have written those songs at any other point in my career; I wouldn't have had the knowledge or the insight or the experience to do it. 1988

'Human Touch' & 'Lucky Town'

If you are trying to cut the records up... there is a lot of groping around on 'Human Touch', less on 'Lucky Town' which is more about finding your place and re-finding yourself, getting back in touch with your own humanity and the good things you find about yourself. Also, there's less fear on that record. Really the records are about – say, if you go back to 'Tunnel Of Love' where the guy in 'Cautious Man' has the words love and fear tattooed on his hands, that's about the story for most people. There's a world of love and there's a world of fear standing right in front of you and very often that fear feels more real, certainly more urgent than the feel of love. 1992

Generally, the imagery is pretty close to the imagery in a lot of my other music. I think that it probably came up out of listening to country music – Hank Williams, Woody Guthrie – where there is a lot of basic imagery, very simple imagery. I guess it's kind of a mythical landscape that everybody carries with them – rivers, forests, sky – they're all very evocative of certain fundamental things. 1992

Specifically I think that you write about the thing that is most urgent to you at any given time and I don't try to connect it completely to my own life in some very specific fashion. I don't think it's like some particular peek – like the guy that does Lifestyle, Robin Leech's territory – into the lifestyles of the rich and famous. I don't think it's like that; I don't think there's anything on there that anybody couldn't really find – with the exception of 'Leap Of Faith'. I was having some fun with it. I guess I put my cards on the table – hey, it's really about just living, love, people trying to connect to each other and that's happening everywhere you know, on any block, every block. 1992

POT-POURRI

What I do is fun and it's brought me a lot of satisfaction. People go about their lives in different ways. They don't get a big fuss made over them but I don't think what I do is any greater – it's just noisier.
1975

I think that all the great records and all the great songs say, 'Hey, take this and find your place in the world. Do something with it, do anything with it. Find some place to make your stand, no matter how big or small it is'. That's a pretty wonderful thing for a record to do, particularly since it only costs about 99 cents. 1975

When the guitar solos went on for too long at the end of the '60s, I lost interest. 1976

I never took the press all that seriously. That stuff is here today gone tomorrow. 1977

There's a million guitar players out there all whacking away... one big drone. So I decided I wasn't going to play unless I had to. 1977

I never drink much. Oh, there was one time. For a while I used to hang out with this really big guy, I mean really big, you know. And together we'd head out to the bars. I was under age but nobody guessed. Anyway, we'd make it to these bars and we'd really shake it down. I had a great time with this big guy. But then I never saw him again. 1978

I like a suit but I don't look right in a suit. I put a suit on, my face just don't go with the suit, man! My face – I just ain't got a suit face. It's too bumpy. Weird. 1975

I don't like pictures. I don't like video tapes. It ain't a natural thing. It's weird, very weird. 1975

There was a piece I read and the only thing that upsets me is the guy, whoever wrote it, couldn't hear what was on the album. To me that was upsetting because I know what's on there, because I died on the damn thing. 1975

All that sort of stuff, if you believe that it has anything to do with you, you know, you're gonna go nuts. In the end, people will like my records and feel they were true, or feel they weren't. They look at the body of work I've done and pull out what ever meaning it has for them. And that's what stands. The rest is meaningless. 1987

There were people who raved about 'Born To Run', people who slammed it. And I was 25, and at that age you're not really sure if what you're doing is any good. Sometimes you wake

up and think, 'This is great.' Other times you think it's garbage – you don't have the confidence at that age. 1987

Everybody is saying that cars and girls are all I sing about! I always like those reviews. It's funny, because I remember when I was about 24 I said, 'I don't want to write about cars and girls any more'. Then I realised, 'Hey! That's what Chuck Berry wrote about!' So it wasn't my idea. It was a genre thing, like detective movies. 1987

I guess I feel like I know a lot more about it than I ever did, but it's like everything else: you gotta write that new song every day. 1988

AMERICA

If you're going to stand up and say, 'I'm an American', that means you've got some responsibility to America.
1975

hard to believe it happens in a country so rich as ours. That's something we ought to be ashamed of. **1985**

After Watergate, America just died emotionally. Nobody had any hope left. People were so horrified when they learned of the large-scale corruption in the land of the brave and the free that they stayed in their houses, scared and numbed. **1985**

Vietnam turned this whole country into a dark street, and unless we can walk down those dark alleys and look into the eyes of those men and women, we are never gonna get home. **1987**

Initially, (the 1992 LA riot) was a funny sort of thing. That particular afternoon in Los Angeles was an afternoon when people were really very frightened; a day when all the invisible walls that were put up in Los Angeles – really a very segregated city – all the invisible walls that were put up started falling, you could feel them beginning to melt away and come down. People

It's like, you gotta watch out – that's the way it's gotta be to get control. All of a sudden you get kids, get them jobs and houses and mortgages and bills, all of a sudden. Jesus Christ, if they don't work they're gonna lose this, they're gonna lose their car, they're gonna lose their house, they're gonna lose their kid, they're gonna lose their money, they're gonna lose their self-respect, they're gonna lose everything. That's how America imprisons everybody. It's like a confining, society-type trip. They imprison you with all these damned goods you know. **1975**

When I was a kid, I think I was afraid of belonging to something because if you admit you belong to something that means you've got some responsibility. If you're going to stand up and say, 'I'm an American', that means you've got some responsibility to America. In this country we've got plenty of things to be proud of and plenty of things to be ashamed of. **1975**

Sometimes it seems like people going hungry is something that happens a long way away. It's

were very frightened. You can go five blocks and you see burned out buildings. It was a very powerful thing. I felt pretty helpless, angry and helpless, but I can't say I'm surprised. Two years ago when *Do The Right Thing* came out people felt that, after reviewing the movie, it would incite riots in the city. Well, if they think that a movie is going to incite riots, then there is obviously cause to riot – it was just a matter of time. If you watch the political situation in the States, people are disgusted with the two party system at the moment. There is nobody that anybody likes; I think people have lost their faith that the government can tackle those problems. It's hard to see if people themselves have the will to sustain the type of effort that might give people a fighting chance at having just some respect and leading a decent sort of life. It's tough, like you have a nice house, a great part of town, you feel frustrated. The days after the riots, you have military helicopters buzzing thirty feet over your backyard every ten to fifteen minutes. It wasn't a surprise – I don't know where it's going to lead. 1992

FRIENDS & COLLEAGUES

Clarence (Clemons) and I are like that (crosses his fingers tightly). His music and my music are ideally suited. We breathe the same thing.
1978

BRUCE ACTS AS BEST MAN AT STEVE VAN ZANDT'S WEDDING.

I want to get girls into the band for the next album because I've got some good ideas which add up to more than just background vocals. But right now I don't have the money to do it. 1974

The band's built to be flexible. That way, if everybody leaves tomorrow or everybody stays it'll work out. You can get mediocre guys and if you have the right arrangements and you know what to do with them you'll still have a good band. 1974

I got some friends. The guys in the band are my friends. I got a girlfriend. That's who I am with most. 1975

Davey (Sancious, keyboard player who played on Springsteen's first two albums) could get off on playing anything. When we first played together, in the 10-piece band, he was a real wild man. He had the rock'n'roll thing in him – it always seemed like he might be the next Jimi Hendrix. He had the potential to be that. 1978

Steve (Little Steven) is a local man. If you keep with the cats around your town and the people that you grew up with, then you maintain your essence. 1975

If you like rock'n'roll, you gotta like our band. The guys have got a great sense of history about

them. We're a real American band; there are practically no European influences. 1978

It's weird because the E Street Band is not really a touring band or just a recording band. And it's definitely me, I'm a solo act you know. 1978

Anybody who works with me, the first thing you better know is I'm going to drive you crazy. Because I don't compromise in certain areas. So if you're going to be in, you better be prepared for that. 1978

And Steve (Little Steven), Steve was known then for practising his guitar, day in and day out,

night and day, all the time. Every time I'd see
him, he would practise, practise, practise. He
always had his guitar with him, everywhere he
went, you know. See him on the boardwalk, he's
always got his guitar with him. Practise, practise,
practise. 1982

I don't hire studio musicians. I don't want guys
with big houses playing for me. I just put an ad
in the paper and people come out and play.
You take a kid off the street and he'll play his
heart out for you. If someone's primarily
interested in how much money's he's going to
make, I don't want him playing for me.
1982

Nils' (Lofgren) guitar always sounded so full. He
is a great guitar player and he just fit in right
away. It was great having him. He's a lot of fun,
especially on stage. 1987

ABOVE: NILS LOFGREN;
BELOW: BRUCE, WITH
RONNIE SPECTOR.

SUCCESS & FAME

I look like, you know, Mr Face-in-the-crowd, that's me! Only place I get recognised if I go out is in a club, but in general the most that happens is somebody comes up and says, 'Hi'.
1975

There is a danger I could be treated like a product instead of a person. I have to be careful. A lot of things are being said about me, and some of them are crazy. 1975

We're driving around and we ain't no phenomenon. The hype just gets in the way. People have gone nuts. It's weird. All the stuff you dream about is there, but it gets diluted by all the other stuff that jumped on you by surprise. 1975

I can't see myself big or a star kind of guy. I mean, ah, not in the normal sense or original sense. Maybe, I don't know. I mean, I gotta good band. I've got some of the greatest guys in the world. 1975

If I was rich? If I made a lot of money you mean? Let me think. Phew! I'd get my mother to quit working. My father to quit working. My mother's been working since she was 18 – she's 50 now. It's too long to work. Right off, that's about all I can think... maybe get an apartment in New York. 1975

I was always the kind of guy who liked to walk around and slip back into the shadows. What you dig is the respect for what you're doing, not the attention. Attention, without respect, is jive. 1977

I looked around and saw all these people who should have been getting something, like my folks or some of the guys who've been with me for years now. I'd like to be able to set them up better. But I will be able to soon. Next year at this time, we may sit in a room like this, and I'll have diamonds on my fingers. But, hey, I've got a car, a motorcycle, a truck, a house... what more could I possibly want? 1977

You ride in a limousine the first time, it's a thrill but after that it's just a stupid car. 1978

I don't know if I can articulate this properly, but this room, and money, it's there, but it's not important. It's not the end. 1981

The sell-out doesn't occur when you take your first limousine ride, it happens in your heart. A lot of good people with something to say have fallen into that trap. It's when you get fat and lose your hunger, that is when you know the sell-out has happened. 1981

Well, see, that particular word... success. It's all down to what you're aiming for. Like, I felt relatively successful when I was just going out and playing the clubs in New Jersey. 1981

I just figure, it's like if you're gonna make more than 500 dollars a night, you're gonna have more than just 500 dollar problems. That's all there is to it. 1981

First the car, the limousine... the big mansions on the hill. I've always been suspicious of the whole package deal and I'm scared of it. I'm afraid because you see so many people getting blown away, getting sucked down the drain. 1981

When all the attention started I was out in LA and Jack Nicholson came to a show. I asked him how he handled the attention. He said for him, it was a long time coming and he was mostly glad to have it. I didn't quite see it that way. I bundled it all together into one general experience and labelled it 'bad'. I felt control of my life was slipping away and that all the attention was, like, an obstacle. 1981

Right after 'Born To Run' I asked myself, 'What do I really want?' I figured I'd better get it straight. I said, 'I want to be a rocker, a musician, not a rock'n'roll star'. There's a difference. The bigger you get the more responsibility you have. So you have to keep constant vigilance. You got to keep your strength up because if you lose it, then you're another jerk who had his picture on the cover. 1982

I don't live that much differently than I did. I still live in New Jersey and I go down the clubs and I play in the clubs all the time. I still see a lot of the people that I always saw. 1984

I got a nice house, I gotta couple of different cars, different old cars and stuff that are fun, but for the most part those things, if they're not distractions… the main thing, the thing that has always meant the most to me, was the performing and the playing and feeling that connection. 1984

The trappings and stuff are a joke. The only fun of sitting in a limousine was if you weren't supposed to be in it. 1985

I used to think that fame, on its best day, is kind of like a friendly wave from a stranger standing

Whatever your recent image is, there are elements of it that is part of who you are, your personality; but a lot of it is some sort of collective imagining that you may have contributed to in some fashion, and in some ways you haven't. It can end up being confining at times and the best thing is to have a lot of holes poked in it – and everybody's always willing to help you out! What I think happens, is that you get into the situation where the myth of success in America is so powerful, that that story can overwhelm or does overwhelm the story that you may think you're telling or may want to tell. Success at that level is a tricky business because

BRUCE, ON STAGE WITH BILLY JOEL (LEFT) AND PAUL SIMON (RIGHT) AT A BENEFIT SHOW FOR HOMELESS CHILDREN AT MADISON SQUARE GARDEN, NEW YORK, IN 1987.

by the side of the road. And when it's not so good, it's like a long walk home all alone, with nobody there when you get there. 1987

When I was young I felt excluded from the community and I wanted to gather people around me, to be part of the community. I thought that by being a musician I would succeed. But the opposite happened: the community gathered around me, or rather around my music, and me, I'm excluded. 1987

I'd like to spend more money, but I don't know how. I have a little house in California and another one in New Jersey. 1987

a lot of distortion creeps in. Not being someone who is a particular 'media manipulator', it was fascinating realising that you really do comment on a lot of different levels – at that level of success. There's the songs you're writing and the things you're telling and then the things that are happening to you; that's also another story! Very often your success story is a bigger story than whatever you are trying to say on stage. That happens a lot here. 1992

BRUCE, WITH FIRST WIFE JULIANNE PHILLIPS.

WOMEN, LOVE & RELATIONSHIPS

I remember the night that I got married. I was standing at the altar by myself, and I was waiting for my wife, and I can remember standing there thinking, 'Man, I have everything. I got it all'.
1987

Man, I couldn't talk to girls at all. Me and Steve (Little Steven) used to sit on my front porch when I lived on South Street in Freehold. Every day at 5 p.m. this girl would walk by and I wanted to go up and talk to her. I'd say to Steve 'Go talk to her, man'. And we'd sit there like two fools. We tried to get the crazy kid on the block to do it for us. 1975

This little girl couldn't have been more than 15 and she had braces on her teeth. And she had her tongue so far down my throat I nearly choked. 1975

I lived with someone once for two years. But I decided that to be married, you had to write married music. And I'm not ready for that. 1975

I can't have any women. I've got to give everything to my music. And I'm not ready to make married music yet. 1975

I guess I'm more of a romantic guy. I don't run around too much. I kinda keep to myself. As a writer it's where you're from. You know, if you grow up in a slum, you just want it like that. You don't show, like, that kind of emotion. To

BRUCE, WITH PATTY SCIALFA, HIS SECOND WIFE, THE MOTHER OF HIS TWO CHILDREN AND OCCASIONAL SINGER WITH THE E STREET BAND.

show too much was not the thing to do in those days. I sort of keep to myself as far as I can. 1975

I was 14 when I first made love. And when I'd done it I didn't know if I'd done it or not. 1978

That's the hardest thing for me to talk about (relationships). I don't know, I'm in the dark as far as all that stuff goes. It took me five albums to even write about it. 1981

Everybody seems to hunger for THAT relationship and you never seem happy without it. I think you do tend to think about that particular thing around 30. But even up till then, when I was writing all the earlier songs, 'Born To Run' and stuff, they never seemed right without the girl. It was just part of wherever that person was going. It wasn't gonna be any good without her. 1981

BRUCE, WITH FORMER STIFF RECORDS SINGER RACHEL SWEET.

The real crazy thing was the wedding. I had planned well and we managed to outwit the press. And suddenly, what do I see on the roof? A seven- or eight-year-old boy shooting photos with his Instamatic. The son of a bitch! Anyway, it didn't make any difference since one of our guests sold his photos to the press. 1987

Gee, there's more to life than this. It's just a cliché, but that, in a funny sort of way, is it. Knowing that there are things I need that can only be provided by people. By contact. By women. By friends. You can't be the guy just blowing the horn on the mountain. 1987

The night my son was born, I probably got as close to the feeling of pure, sort of unconditional love and with all the walls down. All of a sudden, what was happening was so immense that it stopped all the fear for a little while. I remember I was so really overwhelmed with the feeling of the thing but I also understood why you are so frightened, when that world of love comes rushing in, that world of fear comes in with it, whether you got something to lose. If you open yourself up to one thing, you have to face up to another thing; you got to embrace both things and when you embrace both things you're just around that corner from death, the whole bit, the whole nine yards. But it was also something so powerful that my music over the past four or five years has dealt with primitive issues; about someone trying to walk through that world of fear so he can live in the world of love. 1992

I think very few people can confront themselves very accurately. We all live with our illusions and in our own self-image and a good percentage of it is always a bit of a pipe-dream. If you can cut that stuff away a little bit, which is what I have tried to do in my music, and realise I do this well or I am really very bad over here and I'm just taking baby-steps in this part of my life, then it gets you closer to feeling a certain sort of fullness in your life that I always felt like I was missing. I enjoyed my work and everything, but I felt like I couldn't function outside of it. I always had a hard time. 1992

JULIANNE PHILLIPS MODELLING SWIMWEAR.

ENGLAND

What, no hamburgers in London? The tour's off!
November 1975

BRUCE ON STAGE AT THE HAMMERSMITH ODEON IN NOVEMBER, 1975.

I don't think I did so well in England. The first show I did there, I think was one of the worst shows I've ever done in my life. Matter of fact, I know I stunk the first show there. I thought I stunk and I don't think anyone in the band will disagree with me. 1977

At the time of the first London shows I had such a psychic weight on my head – just dealing with myself every day, to get through. I had battles with myself every day, and when I walked out of that theatre in London, I just wanted to go home back to New Jersey. 1977

I felt I was in my 'I Walked Like A Zombie' routine. It was nothing to do with the place. It was me. It was the inside world. It's hard to explain, but I learned a lot about my strengths and weaknesses in those days, especially on that particular night (his first London performance). 1980

London audiences are notorious for being very cool. They check you out very cautiously. 1981

I've always been haunted by the two gigs we played in England in '75. I've got absolute total recall of those shows because the first one was so bad and I was ready to blow up fucking Big Ben. 1981

England is really more fashion-conscious than the States. I play more, I guess, old-fashioned stuff. More straight old-fashioned rock 'n' roll. 1981

HEROES, INFLUENCES & ELVIS

Man, when I was nine, I couldn't imagine anybody not wanting to be Elvis Presley.
1983

BRUCE SHARES THE VOCAL MIKE WITH MICK JAGGER.

I was into The Rolling Stones. I dug the first few Stones albums, the first three or four maybe. 1974

It's funny because I could never really picture Buddy Holly moving. To me, he was always just the guy with the bow tie on the album cover. I liked the film (The Buddy Holly Story) because it made him a lot more real for me. 1975

I was provoked to think by Elvis Presley. He made me think, 'Where am I at?' Dylan, Elvis Presley, Eddie Cochran – these guys provoke thought in me. They give you a little spark; it's fun, it's life – rock and roll. 1975

First record I ever bought, I think, was 'Jailhouse Rock'. 1975

There have been contenders. There have been pretenders. But there is still only one King – Elvis Presley. 1975

When we got to the gate (of Elvis' house), I looked through. It was three a.m. but all the lights in the house were on. I said, 'I got to see if he's home'. So I climbed over and started up the driveway; it's a long walk because the house is set way back. And I was almost at the front door, just getting ready to knock, when I see this guy looking at me from the trees. He says, 'Hey, come here a minute'. I said, 'Is Elvis here?' He said, no, he was in Lake Tahoe or something. Well, now I'm pulling out all the cheap shots I can think – you know, I was on Time, I play guitar, Elvis is my hero, all the things I never say to anybody, because I figure I've got to get a

message through. But he just said, 'Yeah, sure. Why don't you let me walk you down to the gate. You've got to get out of here'. He thought I was just another crazy fan – which I was. 1978

It's just great to front. Like in the early Sixties there were some great front men. Like Paul Jones with Manfred Mann. I always loved that guy, thought he was fantastic. Man, when they came out and did 'Do Wah Diddy Diddy' – I loved them. I love all their songs. I thought he was a great, great singer, Paul Jones. 1978

I like the cat (Bob Dylan) but we came from two totally different scenes, you got to remember that. 1978

I play Buddy Holly every night before I go on, that keeps me honest. 1978

Rock stars, they're just people who wanna crawl back in the womb, people who have built their own reality and are afraid of reality itself. 1978

Sometimes people ask, 'Who are your favourites?' My favourites change. Sometimes it's Elvis, sometimes it's Buddy Holly. Different personalities. For me, the idea of rock'n'roll is sort of my favourite. The feeling. 1978

The Beatles opened doors. Ideally, if any stuff I do could ever do that for somebody, that's the best. Can't do anything better than that. 1978

Bob Dylan's music is the greatest music ever written, to me. The man says it all, exactly the

right way. Incredibly powerful. You don't get no more intense. 1980

I've been influenced by a lot of people. Elvis was one of the first. Otis Redding, Sam Cooke, Wilson Pickett, The Beatles, Fats Domino, Benny Goodman, a lot of jazz guys. You can hear them all in there if you want. 1980

I go back further all the time. Back into Hank Williams, back into Jimmie Rodgers. The human thing that's in those records is just beautiful and awesome. 1980

Here was a guy (Elvis Presley) who had it all and he lost it, or maybe just let it slip through his fingers because somewhere, somehow, he just stopped caring. He let himself get fat and he became a cartoon. 1981

There ain't no more. Everything starts and ends with him (Elvis). He wrote the book. He is everything to do and not to do in the business. 1981

I don't feel that Elvis let anybody down. Personally, I don't think he owed anything to anybody. As it was, he did more for most people than they'll ever have done for them in their lives. 1984

I think about Elvis a lot and what happened to him. The demands that this profession make on you are unreasonable. It's very strange to go out and have people look at you like you're Santa Claus or the Easter Bunny. 1985

It was hard for me to understand that somebody whose music was full of so much life (Elvis') and who'd taken away so many people's loneliness and had given so many people a reason to live, and a look into the promise of life, could have died so tragically. It seemed like such a meaningless death and he deserved a lot better, that's for sure. 1986

I got into this writer, William Price Fox, who wrote 'Dixiana Moon' and a lot of short stories. He's just great with detail. In 'Open All Night' I

remember he had some story that inspired me, I forget what it was. But I was just interested in maintaining a real line through the thing. 1987

Elvis' message was profound. It reaches everybody, everywhere. Doesn't matter where or what the problems are or what the government is like. It bypasses those things. It's a heart to heart. It's a human thing. 1987

The first time that I heard Bob Dylan, I was in the car with my mother and we were listening to, I think, WMCA, and on came that snare shot that sounded like somebody had kicked open the door to your mind... 'Like A Rolling Stone'. And my mother, she was no stiff with rock'n'roll, she used to like the music, she listened, she sat there for a minute and she looked at me and she said, 'That guy can't sing'. But I know she was wrong. I sat there and I didn't say nothing, but I knew that I had

listened to the toughest voice I had ever heard. 1988

When I was a kid, Bob Dylan's voice somehow thrilled me and scared me, it made me feel kind of irresponsibly innocent, and it still does. 1988

The way that Elvis freed your body, Bob freed your mind and showed us that just because the music was innately physical did not mean that it was anti-intellect. 1988

Without Bob Dylan, The Beatles wouldn't have made 'Sergeant Pepper', The Beach Boys wouldn't have made 'Pet Sounds' and The Sex Pistols wouldn't have made 'God Save The Queen'. 1988

Dylan was a revolutionary. So was Elvis. I always saw myself as a nuts-and-bolts kind of person. 1988

THE MUSIC BUSINESS

I never did anything for money, when I was a kid, because I'd seen it kill my old man. Money is a cheap way to get respect.
1978

time. There's too much junk out there already. There's no point in throwing out more junk, you know. 1974

It takes a lot of fun out of it (business). I've got people I pretty much trust. 1975

They probably don't like him (Mike Appel, ex-manager). But, what can I say? I like the guy. I like Mike Appel because he is very responsive. They don't understand. 1975

I've had a million guys come up and say, 'Hey man, let me manage you, put you on tour with The Who, I'll put you on tour with The Rolling Stones, in front of eight billion people, and you'll be famous tomorrow and we'll make a lot of money and be rich. That's not my scene. 1975

Look at us: we've been going for two years and the second record is at 70,000. That's nothing. That really is nothing. That's zero. It depends on who they're dealing with, who they're messing with. It depends on the person. It's like anything – some people can be stopped and other people can't be stopped. I can't stop, they can't make me stop ever, because I can't stop. 1974

We don't make any money off records. We have to go out and play every week, as much as we can. If not, nobody gets paid. In order to maintain and raise the quality of what we're doing, we got to play all the time. 1974

And now they want a single instead of my album. Did they ask Michelangelo to paint them a picture of his parents before he could do the Sistine Chapel? 1974

People run out and say, 'I gotta make a record'. You don't. You make a record when you want to make a record, and when you're ready to make a record. It's been over a year, so what? We just don't run in the studio and waste our

I don't think about anything too much. I don't think about the record industry. I just don't want to know. I'm wary now. I know what I want. I don't wanna be sidetracked with any industry concerns. It's not my deal, it's not the deal I get going. As long as it can be used to the good, that's all that matters. 1975

I decided a long time ago, I know who I am and I know what it is to be caught up in pressure. You start thinking that you're something else. You start becoming a product of the entertainment business. I try to keep my perspective on the thing. It's even for the good of the record company that I do that, because I'll give them my best and it'll work out for the best in the end. 1978

In a way Mike (Appel) was as naïve as me. 'You be the Colonel, and I'll be Elvis'. Except he wasn't the Colonel, and I wasn't Elvis. 1978

I didn't know what (music) publishing was. You're gonna think it's what happens to books. It's one of those words. 1981

He (Mike Appel) worked hard for a long time, we all worked hard, and he sacrificed and okay, he deserved something for it. But what I wanted was the thing itself: my songs. It got so where, if I wrote a book, I couldn't even quote my lyrics – I couldn't quote 'Born To Run'! That whole period of my life just seemed to be slipping out of my hands. That's why I started playing music in the first place – to control my life. No way was I going to let that get away. 1981

When you're up against big business and politics, you gotta have some muscle. 1982

It still puts me straight to fucking sleep, the economic side of things. 1984

The casualty rate in this business is real high. But life is a struggle for most people. It's a thin line between surviving and not making it. It's like people with their finger in the dyke, trying to hold back the flood all the time. That's what our band is all about. 1986

My life was pretty one-dimensional from when I was 14 into my 30s. It was just music, music, music, which was okay, it was good, but, you know, there's other things. 1986

MTV provides all the physical information which is a big part of the rock'n'roll thing. I go over to my friend's house and the kids are glued to MTV. It has taken the place of cartoons for the kids. My attitude is that it reaches a lot of people and I am interested in that field. 1987

On videos there is a basic aesthetic problem when you illustrate a song. People should be allowed the freedom of their own imagination. Say like 'My Father's House', everybody sees a different situation. My songs are full of a lot of cinematic details; when I write a song, that's it. It's meant to evoke personal emotions in the

ABOVE: PATTY SCIALFA, BRUCE AND 'KILLER' JOE DELIA; BELOW: AN AGING BRUCE AS SEEN IN THE VIDEO FOR 'ONE STEP UP'.

listener, so when you do a video you either illustrate the song or you create another story to go over the song and that's silly because there's a story already there that I wanted to tell. 1987

We get approached by corporations. It's just not something that struck me as the thing that I wanted to do. Independence is nice. That's why I started this, for the independence. I'm telling my story out there, I'm not telling anyone else's. I'm saying what I want to say. That's the only thing I'm selling. 1987

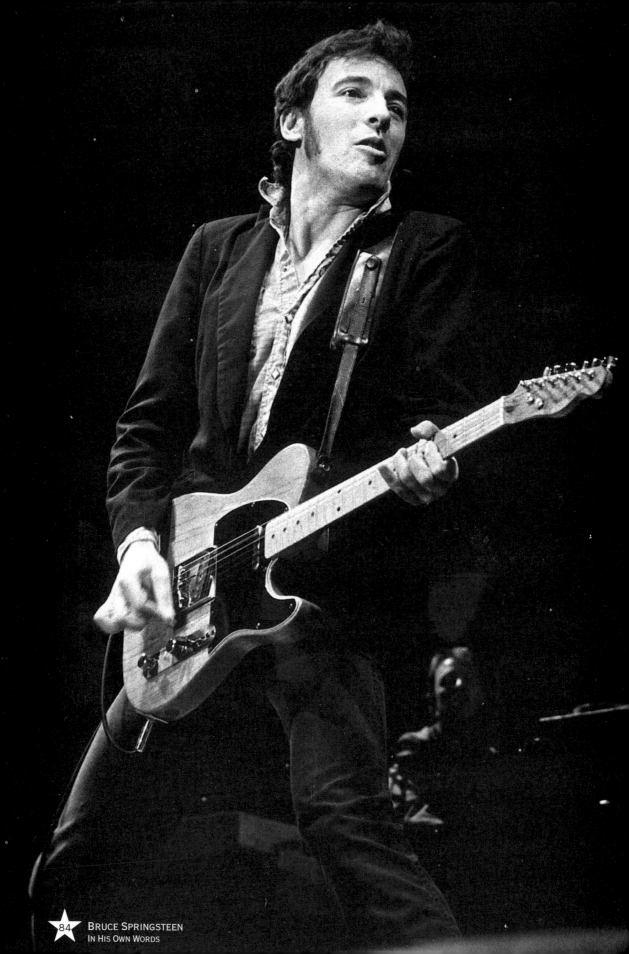

BRUCE SPRINGSTEEN
IN HIS OWN WORDS

POLITICS & RELIGION

THE AMNESTY INTERNATIONAL TOUR LINE-UP: BACK, STING, BRUCE AND PETER GABRIEL; FRONT, TRACY CHAPMAN AND YUSSOU N'DOUR.

There's too much greed, too much carelessness. I don't believe that was ever the idea of capitalism. It's just gotta be voices heard from all places.
1980

I don't go to church. I ain't been to church in eight years. I don't believe in any of that stuff. 1975

I did read the Bible some. I tried to read it for a while about a year ago. It was great. It's fascinating. I got into it quite a ways. Great stories. 1980

It's just the whole thing. It's terrible, it's horrible. Somewhere along the way, the idea, which I think initially was to get some fair transaction between people, went out of the window. And what came in was: the most you can get. The most you can get and the least you can give. 1980

It ain't about two cars in the garage. It's about people living and working together without stepping on each other. 1980

It's disgusting the disrespect those people with responsibility can have. Like TV... there's some good things on TV, but way too much of it is used to zonk people out. 1980

I'm not sure what you think about what happened last night (when Ronald Reagan was elected president), but I think it's pretty terrifying. 1980

There's something really dangerous happening to us out there. We're slowly being split into two different Americas. Things are getting taken from people that need them and given to people that don't need them. There's a promise getting broken. 1980

I don't think the American Dream was that everyone was going to make it or that everyone was going to make a billion dollars. But it was that everyone was going to have an opportunity and the chance to live a life with some decency and a chance for some self-respect. 1980

Things like Watergate – people have lost the ability to dream. It's been knocked out of people. 1981

I was raised Catholic and everybody who was raised Catholic hates religion. They hate it, they can't stand it. 1982

I quit the stuff (religion) when I was in eighth grade. By the time you're older than 13 it's too ludicrous to go along with any more. By the time I was in eighth grade I just lost it all. 1982

I had no political standpoint whatsoever when I was 18, and neither did any of my friends. 1984

The whole draft thing was a pure street thing – you don't wanna go! And you didn't want to go because you'd seen other people go and not come back. The first drummer in a band called The Castiles, he enlisted and he came back in his uniform and it was all, 'Here I go, going to Vietnam', laughing and joking about it. And he went and he was killed. 1984

It wasn't until later, in the 70s, there was this kind of awareness of the type of war it was, what it meant, the way it felt to be a subversion of all the true American ideals. It twisted the country inside out. 1984

And you see the Reagan re-election ads on TV – you know: 'It's morning in America'. And you say, well, it's not morning in Pittsburgh. It's not morning above 125th Street in New York. It's midnight, and, like, there's a bad moon rising. 1984

The president (Ronald Reagan) was mentioning my name the other day and I kind of got wondering what his favourite album must have been. I don't think it was the 'Nebraska' album. I don't think he's been listening to this one (the band then played 'Johnny 99'). 1984

When Reagan mentioned my name in New Jersey, I felt it was another manipulation, and I had to disassociate myself from the president's kind words. 1984

With countries, just like with people, it's easy to let the best bits about you slip away. 1987

We live in times that are pretty shattered. 'I got my music, you got yours, the guy up the streets has his'. And you can kind of sit back, not cynically, but truthfully and say, 'Well maybe all men are not brothers. Maybe we'll never know who or what we are to each other'. 1987

It's sad to think that there's a generation of children out there whose memories of their home is going to be a welfare motel or a shelter. These kids are going to end up living their childhood in what amounts to being refugees in their own land. 1987

I don't like you. I don't like your boss. I don't like what you did. Thank you. (His response to a request from Oliver North's secretary to meet up backstage.) 1988

BRUCE AND STING.

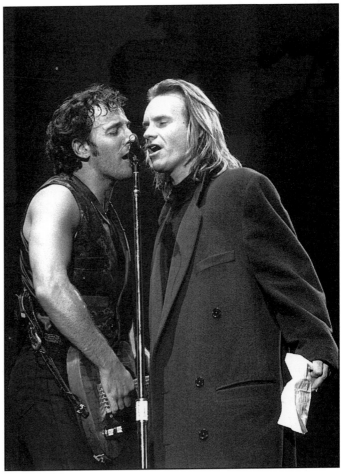

NILS LOFGREN, CLARENCE CLEMONS AND BRUCE.

*Remember, in the end,
nobody wins unless
everybody wins.*
1980

PHILOSOPHY & THOUGHTS

Isolation is the most dangerous thing on earth.
1987

I couldn't bring up kids. I couldn't handle it. I mean it's too heavy, it's too much. A kid – like you better be ready for them. I'm so far off that track. I'm so far out of line, that it would be disastrous. I don't understand it. I just don't see why people get married. I guess it's a nice track, but not for me. 1975

I loved driving around in my car when I was 26 and I'll love driving around in my car when I'm 36. Those aren't irrelevant feelings for me. 1975

In life you've gotta keep yourself bare, you've gotta keep yourself trimmed down. Can't start collecting a lot of junk. I throw out almost everything I own. I don't believe in collecting anything. The least you have to lose the better you are, because the more chances you'll take. 1975

The message in the records is, just follow your heart, as corny as that may sound. There are people trying to hold on to the things they believe in, but it's all very difficult. 1978

The cynicism of the last 10 years is what people adopted as a necessary defence against having tyre tracks up and down their back every day. 1979

There's no place to take aim. There's nobody to blame. It's just things, just the way. Whose fault is it? It's a little bit of this guy, a little bit of this other guy. 1980

To me, the type of things that people do that make their lives heroic are a lot of times very small, little things, little things that happen in the kitchen or something, or between a husband and wife, or between them and their kids. 1980

You don't really know what your values are worth until you test them. So many things happened to me so fast. I always felt if the music was right, I would survive. But if that went wrong, that was the end of it. 1980

I don't have time to read books. You know what it's like. I don't have patience either. That's my problem. If I get into reading them, I like to read them. But I can't sit there and take all them hours reading a book. 1980

You grow up, and they bury you. They keep throwing dirt on you, throwing dirt on and dirt on and dirt on, and some guys they bury so deep they never get out. Six foot, 12 foot down. Other guys, something comes along and they're able to get some of it away. They get a hand free or they get free one way or another. 1980

There's not much people can count on today. Everything has been so faithless, and people have been shown such disrespect. You want to show people that somehow, somewhere, somebody can... you just don't want to let them down. 1981

People get so much shit shovelled on them every day. But it's just important to hold on to those things. Don't let anybody call you foolish. 1981

I will never put someone in the position of being humiliated. It happened to me for far too long. 1981

People never sold out by buying something. It wasn't ever something they bought, it was something that they thought that changed. 1984

You've got to be your own hero, find it out for yourself. I'm only the catalyst. 1984

I think when you're a kid, one of the scariest things is hearing grown-ups argue. 1985

I think you can make anything happen. That's my approach. To blame something on your job is an excuse, no matter what it is. It can make it difficult, no doubt about it. But in the end, you do what you want to do. That's what I basically believe. All the rest is excuses. 1985

Everybody has it but most people just never figure it out. You've got to be able to see yourself for what you are, and not until then can you be what you want to be. 1986

I always wanted to live solidly in the present. When you reach for and achieve fame, one of the by-products is that you will be trivialised. 1987

If you do not develop the skills to interpret information you're going to easily be manipulated, or you're going to walk around simply confused and ineffectual and powerless. 1987

People are being dumped into this incredibly unintelligible society, and they are swimming, barely staying afloat, and then trying to catch on to whatever is going to give them a little safe ground. 1987

I guess when I started in music, I thought, 'My job is pretty simple. My job is I search for the human things in myself, and I turn them into notes and words. And then, in some fashion, I help people hold on to their own humanity – if I'm doing my job right'. 1987

Faith is essential and so is doubt. You are not going to go anywhere with just one of these things, you need them both. Faith, whether it is in a relationship or in your own experience, pushes you onwards and doubt tempers the faith, makes it realistic and pragmatic. It makes you question yourself and sort of investigate what you are doing so you can do it better down the line. 1987

From the beginning there was only one way you could really affect things – through action, through doing something. 1987

I like being on stage when I'm on stage. When I'm not on stage, I don't like being on stage. 1987

You really can't tell people what to hold onto – you can only tell YOUR story. Whether it's to tell it to just one person or a bunch of people. 1987

And my generation, we were the generation that was going to change the world. That somehow we were going to make it less alone, a little less hungry, a little more of a just place. But it seems that when the promise slipped through our hands, we didn't replace it with nothing but lost faith. 1987

I don't believe that you find something and there it is and that's the end of the story. You have to find the strength to sustain it and build on it and work for it and constantly pour energy into it. There's days when you're real close and days when you're real far away. 1988

I think the world is a much harsher place. When you're young you think you will never grow old. That's part of the strength, part of the beauty. 1987

In my business you're afforded the luxury of adolescence and it can go on indefinitely. I think I have gotten very good in my job and because I was very good at my job, for some reason I thought that I would be very capable at other things, like relationships and if you're not, in your twenties you don't really notice it. You're too busy scuffling and as you get a little older you begin to realise "Oh! I see I'm good at this and all these other things I'm bad at, I've been failing miserably at for a long time" and you begin to investigate what those things were; what is basically your real life, your life away from your instruments, your guitar, your music, your work, your life outside your work.

I think in that area, where over the past eight years or so I have been investigating, I really come up short in a lot of ways and so I have just been trying to sort my way through feeling good, whether I've got the guitar on or whether it's in the case.

A lot of the music is focused around what defines my manhood to me, what are my commitments – how to try to stick by them as best as possible, in a world where you really can't know yourself. 1992

TALKING ABOUT BRUCE

When I saw this guy I knew there was something special about him. I knew that he had what it takes. It was what I was looking for.
Clarence Clemons, E Street Band saxophonist, 1987

If I was with Springsteen, his records would be clearer and better and he'd sell five times as many. PHIL SPECTOR, 1975

This Bruce Springsteen stuff drives me crazy. I wouldn't want to be him for all the money in the world. He's good, but he's not that different from a lot of other people out there. I think he's got development to go through. He's nowhere near as good as his hype. STEPHEN STILLS, 1975

STEVE VAN ZANDT, BRUCE AND PATTY SCIALFA.

When Bruce Springsteen sings on his new album, that's not about 'fun', that's fucking triumph, man. PETE TOWNSHEND, 1975

At every date he goes out and sits in every section of the hall to listen to the sound. And if it isn't right, even in the last row, I hear about it and we make changes. I mean every date too. BRUCE JACKSON, SOUND ENGINEER, 1978

In all my years in this business he is the only person I've met who cares absolutely nothing about money. JOHN HAMMOND, COLUMBIA RECORDS' VICE PRESIDENT OF TALENT ACQUISITION, 1978

He's older and wiser but he never strays from his basic values. He cares as much, more, about the losers than the winners. He's so unlike everything you think a real successful rock star would be. ROY BITTAN, E STREET BAND PIANIST, 1981

America's future rests in a thousand dreams inside your hearts. It rests in the message of hope in songs of a young man so many young Americans admire: New Jersey's own Bruce Springsteen. And helping you make those dreams come true is what this job of mine is all about. RONALD REAGAN, 1984

I will always desire to play with Bruce Springsteen. He's the most inspirational, most dedicated, most committed and most focused artist I've ever seen. I like to be around people like that. MAX WEINBERG, E STREET BAND DRUMMER, 1984

He's so good, you really want to hit him now and again. He'd come to rehearsal and he'd write five songs in a day, and he'd do that all the time, whenever he felt like it. LITTLE STEVEN, 1987

From the very first beat it was like magic. It just fell together. MAX WEINBERG, 1987

The first time I saw Bruce he was opening up for Jethro Tull, before he had a record deal. I went to see Bruce because I was singing in that area with different bands and I wanted to get in a good rock band and he had the best rock band. PATTI SCIALFA, 1987

Springsteen calls out to the Philistines of America. And naturally, there is a huge response. MORRISSEY, 1988

I like Bruce: he's a nice, good fucking journeyman, y'know. He ain't no brilliant artist. I've seen the fucking tops work, tops like Joe Tex, Solomon Burke, James Brown, Sam Cooke, Bobby Womack. KEITH RICHARDS, 1988

He represents America the way most Americans perceive themselves and their way of life. But

Disneyland has always been a truer representation of America than Bruce. PATRICIA MORRISON, EX-SISTERS OF MERCY, 1988

Though I like Springsteen, sometimes his songs get misrepresented as Ya Hoo America stuff. That's so disgusting, to see a crowd waving flags and thinking your country is great when you're going through a dangerous period. PETER BUCK, REM, 1988

When the first album came out, I was making $35 a week playing with Bruce. Then it went up to $50 when we did 'The Wild, The Innocent and the E Street Shuffle'. The most I ever got was $110. Bruce was always real straight. The guitars and his songs were all he cared about. He wanted it real bad, and I knew he would go far. VINI LOPEZ, FORMER DRUMMER WITH THE E STREET BAND, AUGUST 1988

I like Bruce. It took me a long time to like him, it's taken the past three years. I think he always manages to produce one dynamite classic per album. JOE STRUMMER, FORMERLY OF THE CLASH, 1988

I was walking through the precinct the other day, and I saw posters saying The Boss was playing live. I thought, 'Oh that's my old boss', 'cos I used to work for a packing factory. FRANK SIDEBOTTOM, FAMILY ENTERTAINER, JUNE 1988

I'm not surprised at all at how big he has become. I'm just very proud of him. For me, it's kind of like the success of a big brother. SUKI LAHAV, FORMER VIOLINIST WITH THE E STREET BAND, AUGUST 1988

The release of the 'Tunnel of Love' album is a more important Catholic event in this country than the visit of Pope John Paul II. REV ANDREW GREELY, AMERICAN PREACHER, 1988